Dr Phil G's

33

TEFL
Top Tips

A Pocketguide

First edition published by Cambridge Academic, The Studio, High Green, Gt. Shelford, Cambridge CB2 5EG.

ISBN 1-903-499-62-3
978-1-903499-62-7

Printed and bound in the United Kingdom by
4edge Ltd, 7a Eldon Way Industrial Estate,
Hockley, Essex, SS5 4AD.

All illustrations done by Ms LI Xiuhui and Mr XIE Yue

Contents

1. Always Respect Your Students...1

2. Develop Your Own Expertise...3

3. Master the Methods 5

4. Mind the Gap...11

5. Overcome Obstacles to Oracy.......................................13

6. Create a Non-threatening Environment.......................15

7. Maximise Speaking Opportunities.................................17

8. Promote Higher Order Thinking Skills.............................19

9. Activate Schemata..21

10. Elicit Ideas, Opinions and Experience........................25

11. Raise Discourse Awareness...27

12. Support Writing through Elicitation..............................29

13. Use Concept Questions and Timelines.......................33

14. Clarify the Conditionals..37

15. Provide Plenty of Practice...39

16. Don't Forget Dialogues..43

17. Play Vocabulary Games...47

18. Teach Real Language...51

19. Beware of the Textbook...53

20. Prompt Pupil Responses...55

21. Give Learners Thinking Time...57

22. Do a Reality Check...59

23. Respond Constructively...61

24. Praise Good Work...65

25. Manage the Classroom Effectively...67

26. Maintain Cooperation...69

27. Engage with Children's Literature...71

28. Bring out the Big Books...73

29. Map out the Follow-up...75

30. Tune into Music...77

31. Cash in on Pop Culture...83

32. Help with Pronunciation...87

33. Treasure the Intangibles...93

Related reading...97

About **Dr. Phil**

Dr. Phil Glenwright (Ed.D, M.Phil, M.A., B.A., Dip.Ed. RSA Dip.TEFL, Dip.Trans) has a long personal history in language teaching. He started his professional life in 1969 as a German teacher at the curiously named Sexey's School (for Boys) in rural Somerset. He then enjoyed a three year stint as TEFL teacher at a German Grammar School (1971-4) before accepting the post of Head of Languages at a large Comprehensive in Scarborough (1974-8).

After a further year in his beloved Germany (1978-9), he moved into tertiary education as Senior Lecturer in Modern Languages at the then College of St Paul and St Mary in Cheltenham. In 1987 his career swung firmly towards TEFL when he was appointed Senior Lecturer in English in Hong Kong where he has remained ever since. He has published on a variety of subjects in respected journals such as *Education and Society* and the *Journal of Language, Identity and Education*. He is the author of *'The Hong Kong Culture of Learning: Its Origins and Effects'* (2010).

This new book of thoughtful TEFL tips is therefore able to offer a wealth of insights into ESL/EFL teaching which will be of interest both to experienced colleagues, relative newcomers to the profession and to teachers in training, especially those in outer circle and periphery countries where English is a second or foreign language. The book touches on many key TEFL areas but its particular concern is *student oral participation*.

This book is dedicated to all the kind, friendly students – young and not so young – I have taught in schools and universities in England, Germany and Hong Kong

1 Always Respect Your Students

Teachers need to respect and value their students. Not because this has been decreed by academics but because it is essential to effective functioning in the classroom. Teachers who build up the self-esteem and confidence of students, helping them to grow in terms of knowledge and as a person, are far more likely to make a lasting impact on their charges than those who merely want to demonstrate their own authority through negative comment and actions. Being constructive and helpful is, however, not just good from the human perspective, it also fosters a collaborative classroom culture where teachers and students work together to achieve common goals. Significantly, respect for students is based not on some vague do-gooding instinct but on strong scientific evidence regarding people's capacities for learning and retention, described on occasion as almost magically unlimited.

Language learning at school results from a complex amalgam of interrelated factors such as age, personality, motivation, learning styles and intelligence. Some may incline the learner towards the more formal or analytical aspects of study, others may promote a freer, more adventurous spirit and a willingness to try things out orally – to take risks. A sensitive teacher, aware of individual differences as well as group dynamics, can take these factors into account and create the type of environment that is accommodating and secure yet challenging and engaging. In such a setting, almost all learners can achieve a good degree of success with a second or foreign language. Intelligence, however measured and defined, is not the determining factor. It may enhance performance with reading and writing tasks but have less impact in regard to listening or speaking activities. Indeed, since the idea that IQ is fixed at birth has been largely discredited, the emphasis is now on life-long learning and development – there is no restrictive ceiling pre-determined by birth.

Most importantly perhaps, teachers need to be cognisant of the often varied and unsuspected gifts that students may possess. Evidence from work on multiple intelligences indicates that, beyond the traditional, culturally delimited realms of literacy and numeracy, students may possess emotional, artistic, sporting, musical and/or other forms of intelligence which will enable them to function happily and successfully in the adult world. Such gifts may occasionally surface in language classes when project work is undertaken. In any case, it is wise to remember that high levels of academic attainment are not always a pre-requisite for genuine real world achievement. For all these reasons, teachers should adopt a personal professional philosophy that both respects the students and is fundamentally optimistic in outlook.

2 Develop Your Own Expertise

Nobody is quite sure why some teachers stand out from the crowd but many people can remember a special teacher who significantly influenced their life.

One key factor is usually considered to be a love of subject. Teachers who love their subject are usually immersed in it, respect it and steep themselves in knowledge of it. They do not allow students to disparage it or waste precious learning time in class. Language teachers have particular responsibilities in this respect since they speak or model the target language, embody the foreign culture and represent its people(s) in the classroom. Their depth of knowledge, their personal enthusiasm for and wish to integrate with - or at least get to know – others of different nationality, race or religion is crucial and this consequently engenders in them a richer, more critical sense of identity and self.

Pedagogical skill is another important factor contributing to teacher expertise. It is one thing to know your subject, it is quite another to teach it well. The important thing is not perhaps rigid adherence to any particular methodology but an understanding of the benefits and potential pitfalls of differing approaches. Certainly classroom practice should be well informed by theory and *vice versa* but the essential thing is for language teachers to have at their disposal a wide range of teaching approaches and techniques to fit almost every situation. Students are certainly not impressed if teachers are confined to the (often

3

dull) textbook. They are impressed if the teacher has some lively, interactive routines and activities that go far beyond it. Teachers should be eclectic. Where technology is available, its judicious use is also welcomed. The advice would therefore be to constantly update and add to the personal pedagogical repertoire through whatever suitable teacher education offerings are available, through interaction with fellow professionals and also through individual personal initiative.

Perhaps the most important factor of all in teacher expertise is human relations, something that is difficult to legislate for. Whereas knowledge of subject and pedagogical skills may be deliberately acquired, human relations – the ability to strike a resonant chord within the learner and to establish a warm, sincere and lasting rapport both with the class and the individuals in it – comes not so much from the head as from the heart. It may spring from the respect discussed above and/or from a sense of care and understanding which may be imparted in often imperceptible ways. It may even stem from light and spontaneous humour, as with the smiling production of a 'yellow card' (football) to admonish a late arrival in class.

These things are instinctive and relate to individual personality. Indeed, since teachers and teaching styles are as diverse and complex as learning ones, the advice might just be to live and learn, to trust yourself and act naturally. Certainly the combination of love of subject, pedagogical expertise and good human relations is a winner.

3 Master the Methods

While it is best to be eclectic in the selection of teaching approaches, a reasonably sound understanding of the possibilities is helpful. This is not difficult to achieve. Five methods are therefore briefly outlined below.

The traditional or grammar-translation method was prevalent in UK grammar schools in the 1950s but its residual impact may well linger in selective, elitist systems around the world. It is a method devoid of theoretical underpinnings, educational, psychological, linguistic or otherwise. It involved much talk about language, often in L1, much memorization and an almost exclusive focus on writing. Language was viewed as knowledge rather than skill, grammar being taught prescriptively as rules and exceptions to be learnt and memorized by rote. Textbook chapters usually started with an artificially contrived, unnatural presentation passage of limited truth value which served merely to display a particular structure and was populated only by cardboard characters as unreal as the language model itself. The overt top-down teacher explanation of the given points, often couched in complex linguistic terminology, was then followed by exhaustive banks of manipulative, accuracy focused exercises meant to test or trap the unwary in order to prepare them for the ensuing high stakes examinations. This preoccupation with sentence and form resulted in syllabuses that comprised only a lock-step march through the entire range of grammatical structures. Teaching itself was undemanding, since the classroom procedures were teacher, test and textbook-centred and involved a largely transmissive, lecturing style. Frequently therefore L2 students knew the rules but were unable to speak, the direct inverse of native speaker achievement.

Behaviourism in the 1960s and '70s brought a somewhat more balanced approach with emphasis not just on writing but on Listening, Speaking, Reading and Writing – a significant advance. Speech was now classified as the primary skill while descriptive grammars identified the salient functions of real language use. The audio-lingual and audio-visual courses of the time enshrined the prevalent notion that language learning was merely a process of habit formation achieved through analogy, imitation and frequent repetition. The new availability of cassette recorders and language laboratories consequently led to a heavy emphasis on controlled, sometimes drill-like, practice activities focused heavily on accuracy and the avoidance of risk and error. The quality of materials varied. At best spoken contextualized presentation materials had strong elements of authenticity. At worst the practice drills were mechanical and meaningless and could be chanted off sentence by sentence without thought.

Communicative language teaching, which came to the fore in the 1970s and '80s, put a far greater emphasis on the message-oriented functions or purposes for which language is used – together with the need to communicate appropriately (not just grammatically) in real life social situations. Moreover, the brain was now conceived as an innate Language Acquisition Device, pre-programmed to pick up language naturally through exposure to authentic, comprehensible input. Indeed, the mistakes made by young children in L1 (such as '*I goed/I wentid*') indicated that hypotheses about language are formed and tested unconsciously, then being refined not by explanation but through the assimilation of yet further comprehensible input. In consequence great emphasis was placed on interactive fluency-oriented production activities, such as information gap, mingle, surveys and role play, which permitted risk-taking. The language agenda (often a single structure) for these activities was, however, still largely pre-determined by the syllabus or teacher and the supposedly authentic exchanges were therefore sometimes considered only to involve learners in an extended fantasy.

Task-based learning then shifted the goalposts, making the need for worthwhile learning (not language) the number one priority. Focusing on an interesting topic or theme learners are now intended to communicate to learn – not learn to communicate – being involved in purposeful life-like tasks or activities that have both a process of thinking and doing, and a product. The approach, often articulated in a pre-, while- and post- classroom format, embodies a constructivist approach to learning where students build on their existing congruent knowledge.

Simultaneously, language scaffolding or support from competent others, such as teachers or peers, assists them to successfully learn more than might have been achieved in isolation.

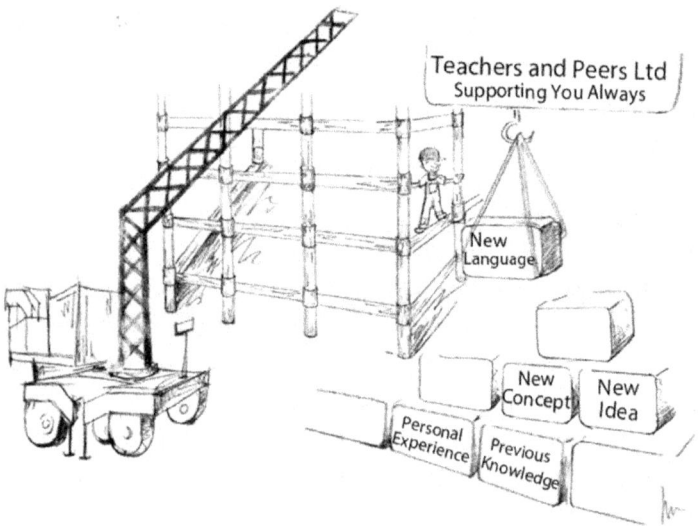

Language, of course, remains essential to the achievement of the broader educational goals and students are encouraged or guided to notice, enquire about and explore the language items essential to the fulfillment of task. The authenticity or semi-authenticity of task materials also ensures an emphasis on meaning, function and discourse (rather than form, structure and sentence). However, where a government syllabus is involved, teacher and learner autonomy may still be subjugated to examination requirements with pedagogical changes remaining somewhat cosmetic.

Post-methods approaches may therefore be less constrained by theoretical imperatives, it being quite impossible to prove by research that one teaching method is superior to some other. There are simply too many variables, and in any case post-modernism is characterized by the denial of any objective truth. The teaching here may therefore involve only a series of well-conceived steps that lead to the achievement of some worthwhile and achievable interim goal or outcome.

4 Mind the Gap

Theory and practice are mutually complementary. The one should inform and exemplify the other. This should be evident in approaches to the teaching of grammar. Presumably few teachers today would wish to adopt the traditional approach to grammar, using uninteresting display texts remote from reality where authors contrive to generate an unnatural abundance of target structure examples, followed by explanations couched in terminology far more abstract and difficult than the actual items themselves.

Two unfortunate examples might be cited here. Firstly, the structure 'used to' might be said – accurately but incomprehensibly to young pupils – to *'denote repeated habitual actions in the remote past'*. Secondly, a traditional treatment of the passive might involve only exercises that concentrate on the meaningless manipulation of form. In this case, highly unlikely utterances such as *'I eat the apple. The apple is eaten by me'* might be the starting point for a series of intricate juxta-positionings and fine re-adjustments to a further series of such abstruse sentences.

A more current approach to these items might involve students in discovering or noticing an occasional example of the 'used to' structure within the context of an authentic passage, story or research project on elderly people, such as grandparents. The teacher might then enable the learners to grasp the particular purpose or function of this item by posing a series of simple concept questions whose easy answers allow learners themselves to define the function: *Are we talking here about the past or the present? Was it last week or a long time ago? Did s/he do it once or often? Can s/he still do it now?* Since some languages have no tense system, understanding the function of each and every tense is extremely helpful.

As for the passive, this might be presented through an authentic newspaper report of a car accident where examples are likely to occur naturally, for example: *An elderly man was hit by a car on Waterloo Rd last night. He was taken to hospital and...* Here once again the function of the passive might be elicited from students by asking why the text does not read: *A brand new Mercedes 280SL hit an old man on Waterloo Rd last night.* Through discussion, it should then be possible to establish that one purpose of the passive is to focus on the victim (not the doer/car).

All this neatly illustrates the well known functional systemic grammar adage that a choice made in form is a choice in meaning. It also confirms that grammar operates in the service of meaning – and not as a form of mental gymnastics – and it makes plain that rules should derive from authentic instances of real language use. Certainly, so-called 'good' grammar teaching focuses on meaning and use whereas 'bad' grammar teaching involves only the pointless manipulation of form.

5 Overcome Obstacles to Oracy

In many foreign language classrooms around the world, learners often appear shy, embarrassed and reluctant to speak, especially perhaps adolescent males. These inhibitions have a number of possible causes, which teachers can both understand and counteract.

Oral anxiety occurs whenever speaking in English appears both frightening and difficult. Even teachers sometimes imply that taking an oral turn in class requires great courage, repeatedly exhorting students to *'Be brave. Try to speak in English'* and/or to *'Speak louder'*. This problem is much exacerbated if learners feel vulnerable and are frightened of making mistakes, perhaps fearing ridicule from the teacher or being mocked or laughed at by classmates.

Cultures of learning (despite dangers of over-generalisation) too may create conflicting expectations. 'Western' teachers, for instance, may be steeped in skill-based 'learning by doing' approaches that emphasise interactive, learner-centred, task-based approaches whereas certain learners, by contrast, may regard language learning as the diligent accumulation of knowledge silently assimilated from authoritative sources such as the teacher and textbook. These differing concepts and expectations concerning the nature of education and learning can spark discord.

Differing communication styles may likewise have an impact, since different societies have varying concepts of power and authority. 'Western' teachers may greatly value verbal fluency whereas learner priorities may emphasise the preservation of social harmony, hierarchy and face and consequently restrict voluntary contributions not sanctioned by the group. Indeed, there may be a tradition of superior (here the teacher) speaking and the inferior (the learner) listening. Assertiveness and eloquence might therefore be considered disrespectful or even impertinent whereas the ability to listen with full attention may be rewarded, authority figures sometimes favouring restrained, tentative and hesitant speech in subordinates.

Textbooks and traditional teaching approaches that offer outdated or inadequate models of language and language teaching may also restrict pupil participation, for instance through an excessive focus on isolated structures, a neglect of collaborative pair and group work and/or a flawed model of spoken English.

6 Create a Non-threatening Classroom Environment

The obstacles identified above can be countermanded. The teacher's own attitude to mistakes is, of course, crucial. Mistakes may generally be regarded as natural, inevitable, helpful and even as a sign of progress. They are an integral part of the learning process and offer the teacher insights into what has not yet been assimilated and suggest ways of offering further helpful input. They are certainly not a sign of shame or failure. Whether or not mistakes are corrected immediately or at some later point in a lesson, whether they are corrected directly through overt explanation or whether the utterance is simply reformulated, recast or paraphrased by the teacher will depend upon the type and stage of an activity and its accuracy or fluency-oriented purposes. Sometimes mistakes are simply ignored.

Explicit correction of mistakes certainly has value since it reveals how language does *not* function but this must be accomplished with tact and good grace through specific, factual and helpful feedback rather than negative comment or vague admonishments to *'be careful', 'work harder'* or *'spend more time'*. Teachers must also challenge any student who laughs derisively at the mistakes of others and must explain the reasons why such behavior is not only unkind and unacceptable but is at odds with current views of how languages are learnt. It is apparent that the teachers' own classroom language, their skill in providing learning and speaking opportunities and, even more, their underlying teaching philosophy will greatly affect the way pupils perceive the classroom and how they react to it.

The primary aim, therefore, is to create a secure, supportive, non-threatening and busy working atmosphere with firm, friendly encouragement so that pupils may feel happy and confident using English from the moment they enter school. It is certainly not easy to learn a second or foreign language without a positive attitude towards the language, the people and the culture. In and often outside the classroom, the teacher is the *de facto* representative of this language and is responsible for creating a positive ambiance towards the outside English-speaking world. It would be ideal if – after a lively very first lesson – the children go home and tell their parents '*I can speak English*' and/or '*I like English*'. A low affective filter facilitates language learning.

At the same time, 'Western' teachers can inform themselves about differing long-established and highly esteemed conceptions of education, learning and the norms of communication that may pertain in unfamiliar cultural contexts, can develop empathetic understandings of such phenomena and yet be ready and able to explain, discuss and justify preferred approaches and their likely perceived benefits. Textbooks and teaching approaches can then be adapted to the extent possible. Missionary zeal is not appropriate but tolerance, cooperation and enthusiasm help.

7 Maximise Speaking Opportunities

Oral proficiency is a vital goal for English learners, especially since (as already noted) speaking is often considered the primary skill which very young children master (unconsciously) in their L1 through immersion – without any explicit instruction but with constant encouragement from parents and care takers.

In the world of formal education, however, classroom students frequently have limited experience of using spoken English, especially in active, questioning roles, spending the majority of their time listening to the teacher. Yet the scientific data clearly indicate that frequent speaking opportunities represent the crucial ingredient in promoting both student confidence and high overall language proficiency levels. Not only therefore does good oral work foster the ability to function effectively in the real world, it also helps learners do better in examinations.

One main objective of TEFL teachers, therefore, must be to maximise classroom speaking opportunities within a non-threatening environment in order to reduce pupil oral anxiety and consequent reluctance to speak. The provision of individual speaking opportunities is therefore a pressing teacher concern. Questioning should, however, be questioned. It need not always be conducted by the teacher. Students themselves can devise lines of enquiry they might wish to pursue with a new topic. Nor need questions always be put to individuals – students can perhaps consult in pairs or groups before reporting to the class, so reducing stress.

Nevertheless questioning in most lessons is likely to be directed by the teacher to the learners so that an examination of question types (and of turn taking) is opportune. One classification is 'open' (with various possible answers) or 'closed' (with only one correct answer). Another is 'referential' (where the teacher does not know the answer in advance) and 'display' (where the student is simply required to furnish knowledge already well known to the teacher in order to demonstrate linguistic facility). Clearly referential/open questions are likely to be more productive, permitting longer, richer and more informative responses.

'Yes/no' questions are, by contrast, extremely limiting, even the answer *'No'* appearing unlikely in instances such as the following: *'Class. Today we will read a story about picnics. Do you like picnics?'* Few willing students would wish to upset the teacher's carefully laid plan! Either/or, Wh- and tag questions are also in common classroom use, as well as declarative statements that (through rising intonation) function as questions.

Given that teacher talk is often estimated to occupy some 70% of lesson time or more, use of the more productive question types is important whilst turns should be well distributed to all areas of the classroom without gender or other bias. The teacher may use 'general solicits' *(Can anyone tell me…)* to elicit responses, or nominate a particular learner to answer after first posing the question. S/he may also direct questions to a learner who *self-selects or bids* for a turn, for instance by raising a hand, occasionally re-directing the same question to a further student either as a check on comprehension or on attention. It is important, however, not to rely solely on volunteers.

8 Promote Higher Order Thinking Skills

The types of questions already discussed are important weapons in a teacher's armoury, though 'open' and 'referential' questions are often sadly underrepresented. Since the teacher 'owns the rights' to questioning, usually nominates the topic and can dictate which knowledge is deemed acceptable, such questioning routines tend to result in a pattern of interaction common in didactic discourse, namely *Initiation* (the teacher asks the question), *Response* (the learner answers) and *Feedback* (where the teacher evaluates and comments on the pupil effort). This sequence, quite rare in everyday conversational exchanges, indicates likely teacher dominance. It can, however, sometimes be mitigated by the more natural, spontaneous interpersonal exchanges that occasionally intersperse lessons.

Given the increasingly sophisticated nature of global interchange and the preponderance of the service industries in advanced economies, there is inevitably a demand for good communication and problem-solving skills (especially perhaps in genuinely democratic societies). Such accomplishments can be fostered not only through referential questions (as above) but also by employing lines of enquiry that demand thinking skills of a higher order.

Here Bloom's (1956) taxonomy appears to have withstood the test of time. He suggests that knowledge *(Where is London?)* and comprehension *(Is it true that... Did they buy*

X or Y?) questions of the type that very frequently accompany presentation or comprehension passages in textbooks involve only low level thought processes. Medium level application *(The clever cat caught the mouse by saying 'squeak squeak'... How would he catch a bird?)* and analysis *(Which are the traditional elements in this story and which are modern?)* questions go a step further whilst synthesis *(Can you put it all together and come up with one new word that captures the essence of the whole story?)* and evaluation *(In your judgement how far/to what extent...?)* ones are the most worthwhile and challenging. They are higher order questions.

Indeed, with so-called listening and reading comprehension passages, such intermediate and higher order questions might fit neatly into the while- and post- reading phases: the medium level ones requiring close intellectual scrutiny of the passage and the higher level ones demanding a creative or evaluative response that transcends the text (in conjunction perhaps with the creation of a poster, article, diary or interview and the expression of opinion).

Other good questioning options exist. Inferencing questions *(As he looked down at the valley the people seemed like ants... Where was he?)*, provenance questions *(Where would you probably find a passage like this?)*, figurative questions *(What does 'The King saw red' mean?)* and those requiring an imaginative response *(So, what would you have done in that situation?)* are also potentially productive in terms of both language and thought.

It is generally good to value elicited pupil ideas by writing key words and ideas on the board. These then provide both lexical and conceptual support.

9 Activate Schemata

A central tenet of constructivism, a socio-cultural theory, is that students accommodate new insights, knowledge and skills into their existing frameworks of knowledge through shared processes of enquiry, thinking, problem-solving, creating, performing and communicating through collaborative classroom activities with strong social or group work components, doing this in ways that are interactive, cyclical and holistic.

Children and young people are definitely not blank slates *(tabular rasa)* to be written on. They live in the real world and know a very great deal about it, about birthday parties, transport systems, cultures and lifestyles and so on. To engage and motivate students, it is therefore essential to tap such personal knowledge and experience by activating their mental schemata through elicitation questions related to the topic or theme in hand. Many textbook topics are good ones, being age appropriate, interesting and potentially meaningful, offering scope to build on and extend congruent student knowledge and real-life experience. Language, for example the present simple tense, is, however, *not* a topic!

Students' mental schemata or frameworks of pre-existing knowledge may be activated from the start of a lesson, especially when launching a new topic. Indeed, interest might be heightened by maintaining an element of suspense so that pupils cannot immediately predict the development and progress of the entire lesson. (Parents/private tutors who preempt texts may make this difficult to achieve). Still, some degree of unpredictability may encourage a greater variety of responses. A three phase lead-in to the topic that possesses a general focus (surveying a whole area from a broad perspective), an intermediate focus (identifying and probing the particular topic area in more detail) and a personal focus (relating the topic to the individual), may be of assistance.

For instance, if a class is later to read a robbery story or article, the teacher might offer some opening statement praising (for example) Hong Kong as a particularly modern and safe city. Thereafter s/he might then ask a question with a broad Hong Kong focus – *What are the biggest problems in HK?* – with many suggestions forthcoming. The intermediate questions might then focus on crime – *Who protects us from bad men/women/ criminals?* The personal focus might then zoom in on the pupils' own life – *How does your family protect itself from thieves?* The intention would clearly be to involve many pupils in speaking, to activate schemata and to access their real world knowledge.

Each of these questions has many potential answers, offering good scope for pupils to speak. They might mention *a) housing, pollution, unemployment, over-crowding, traffic b) policemen/women, customs officials, teachers, parents* and *c) security guards, cameras, locks/grilles on doors, bars on windows.* They may not, of course, use these particular words. They might, for instance, say the *air is dirty* rather than talking about *pollution.* In any case this kind of foundation work facilitates the ease with which subsequent texts may be processed.

10 Elicit Ideas, Opinions & Experience

People talk blithely about elicitation yet may disregard its abiding significance, merely assigning a few perfunctory questions to the opening stages of lessons.

A fundamental principle of teaching today must be to engage students repeatedly in on-going oral interactions with each other and the teacher. The purposes of having a student-centred opening exchange are to:

○ establish English as the natural language of the classroom;

○ involve the pupils at once in genuine (somewhat unpredictable) communication;

○ foster pupil-teacher rapport;

○ permit the teacher to get to know the learners as individuals (rather than numbers);

○ allow the teacher to show interest in pupils' experiences through *follow-up* questions;

○ value pupils' knowledge and experience (perhaps by writing their key points and ideas on the whiteboard);

○ activate the mental schemata necessary for effective learning;

○ convey high, positive expectations of pupils' capabilities;

○ generate ideas and language (not merely one obvious/ correct answer);

○ empower students by giving them a classroom voice;

○ revise and re-work previously learnt or acquired language;

○ create a relaxed, non-threatening atmosphere;

○ set the tone for all that follows;

○ above all to be genuinely interested in and concentrate on the real-life topics (meaning), not merely on some prescribed grammatical structure (form).

Demotivation	Motivation
negative assumptions/ expectations;	positive assumptions/ expectations;
limiting/closed questions;	simple, open, empowering questions;
low truth value;	real-world knowledge and ideas;
interest in form not meaning;	topic-centred opportunities for both thought and communication;
few opportunities for involvement;	many opportunities for Ss involvement;
students' experience/ knowledge neglected;	students' experience and knowledge sought and valued;
authoritarian – learners as numbers;	democratic – interest in individuals;
few ideas and little language generated;	opportunities to express ideas and to communicate;
teacher-centred and impersonal;	student-centred;
likely failure;	likely success;
demotivation.	motivation.

11 Raise Discourse Awareness

Elicitation is clearly a way of bringing learners into the learning arena, creating opportunities both for participation, discovery and the co-construction of knowledge. Apart from accessing learners' real world knowledge and experience in relation to a particular theme or topic, elicitation can engage learners in an on-going 'classroom conversation' that makes explicit the salient discourse features of the text-types they may commonly encounter. These may be either spoken or written.

If, for instance, it is intended to listen to a TV weather forecast, many questions can be posed to activate relevant schemata: *At what times do you see the weather forecast on TV? Is the presenter male or female? Young or middle aged? Sitting or standing? What do you see behind the presenter? What will the presenter talk about first? What else...? What visuals or symbols are used?* There may even be an amusing cartoon animation to finish the broadcast that the teacher can imitate for fun.

It might also be interesting to compare BBC weather forecasts with their closer attention to gender, ethnic and linguistic diversity with local ones in whatever country. In any case, once awareness has been drawn to features such as temperatures, humidity levels and the like, the task of processing the information contained in any following weather forecast will be far easier.

With written genre a similar procedure can be adopted. For example, elicitation questions can draw learners' attention to the discourse features and information structure of a newspaper report. *What do we call the words in large print above the article? Is there a picture? What is the caption under the picture? Is the article written across the page or in columns down it? Are the paragraphs long or short? How about the sentences? Are there more simple, compound or complex sentences? What is the function of the opening paragraph? Are there any witness statements regarding the incident or any official rebuttals from authority figures or spokespersons? What is fact and what is opinion? Does the writer indicate her/his own judgement or perspective through a concluding remark? Which is the main tense?* These types of question (the suggestions are indicative only) draw out certain key aspects of newspaper reports and would help learners to write similar pieces.

More advanced learners might then examine differences in the treatment of a particular news item in the popular and in the more serious press, perhaps approaching these from a critical media awareness perspective and considering issues such as the intended audience, objectivity and bias and the creation and/or elimination of prejudice. Through work on discourse and genre learners may come to appreciate how narrative, procedural, persuasive, expository and/or explanatory texts work, perceiving also whether these involve comparison, cause and effect, lists and descriptions or problems and solutions. Coherence, a macro feature, and cohesion, a micro one, can be explored.

12 Support Writing through Elicitation

Writing is an activity that not all pupils enjoy, so it is important to provide adequate support both in terms of content and language. This will avoid excessive, depressing error where work is returned covered in a sea of red ink with learners consequently resorting to defensive writing. What learners really need is repeatedly experienced success.

There are, of course, many approaches to writing. Process writing, for instance, involves a sequence of: topic selection; pre-writing activities (such as brainstorming); composing (getting initial thoughts onto paper); teacher and/or peer response to the draft (with comments on ideas, organization and style); revisions to the draft with possible further peer review; proofreading and editing to check and correct the language and layout; and publication or display to add a sense of realism and achievement.

Some things, however, appear important whatever the approach. There should be an audience, a purpose and a text-type, for example an email to a friend to arrange a get-together. In real life we certainly do not write 5 sentences merely to display our knowledge of a particular tense! Once such fundamentals are established, interesting ideas may be elicited and shared. Indeed a menu of possibilities may be created on the whiteboard by recording student suggestions and capturing useful expressions and key vocabulary from which learners may later select when they write. This scaffolds students' writing and reduces anxiety and error.

Writing may also be conducted as a group activity. If, for instance, an intermediate class had read a story or seen a film about time travel, an imaginative teacher might devise a scenario where weary time travellers report their difficulties to and seek advice from a Father Time figure in a notional Out of Time magazine. Here again elicitation questions could first establish who – in the real world – might seek advice, what the problems might be and where help could be obtained.

A sample problem letter to Father Time (perhaps with some invented dates such as TimePoint 20.78.90.9) might then be presented to the class with groups consulting and then suggesting their solutions. Next, Father Time's own response might be shown with consequent discussion as to who offered the best response to the problem. Thereafter students might operate in 8 or 10 groups of four, responding to other problem letters from other time travellers sent to Father Time.

To heighten later interest two groups (sitting far apart in the classroom) might tackle the same letter. After drafting, revision and editing, groups addressing the same problem might in turn present their respective solutions via an overhead transparency (OHT), the visualiser or the computer. The primary focus would then be on meaning, on the validity of the proffered solutions, their originality and even perhaps their humour. Attention to form might occur through follow-up comments with final edited versions published in a special second edition of the Out of Time magazine. Such practices are again broadly in line with and informed by theory.

13 Use Concept Questions and Timelines

A 'golden rule' for oral work might, as the heavy emphasis on elicitation suggests, be: *Don't tell. Ask!* The same applies in regard to grammar where students can be guided to notice and/or discover the functions of different tenses which they encounter in some life-like context – as with the previous example 'Used to'. These concept questions are familiar to many teachers but do not always find their way into classroom practice.

With the present continuous the key question to ask is *'Is s/he doing it NOW?'* With the present simple that same question might be repeated (this time eliciting a negative response) and be followed as appropriate by *'Does s/he do it every day/week etc.?'* or *'Is it always true?'* In this way it could be established that the present continuous is used for things happening now while the present simple describes regular or routine actions and/or is used to convey universal truths.

An unwanted and rather crass teacher-centred example of telling rather than asking could be cited here with the simple past where an uninformed teacher might provide highly unlikely invented examples such as *'Class, last week I went to France to go shopping. Last month I went to England to see friends. Last year I went to China to see the Great Wall.'*

Clearly, it would be better to provide a contextualized example (perhaps from a narrative story) and to ask first if the action is happening now or happened in the past and if there is a time word to indicate this. The vital concept question is then *'Is the event/action completely over and finished?'* since describing such completed events represents the function of this tense.

The notion of time as a linear concept in Western societies (it is circular in some) with the future ahead and the past behind can then be discussed and illustrated, a single cross marking the spot where last week's completed event occurred. This makes the concept of the tense immediately visible to learners so aiding deeper understanding.

Other tenses lend themselves to similar timeline treatment. In the case of the past continuous teachers might ask *'Had s/he started watching TV when...? Had s/he finished watching TV when...?'*. In this case the corresponding representation for the continuous element might be a wavy line in the past with a superimposed cross added to denote the sudden, interrupting event, such as a phone ringing.

The present perfect too offers interesting possibilities, the key concept being *'Up to now'*. The likely questions might therefore be *'When did you start playing the piano?'* and *'Are you still doing it today?'* Attention could also be drawn to indicative words such as *'Since 1987/For 30 years'* which denote a point or period of time respectively.

As regards the timeline an arched arrow can link the start of the action in the past to the present point *Now*. Teachers may also draw attention to the fact that the timeframe from past to present could cover thousands of years (or more) or just a few minutes.

A *Curriculum Vitae* or *Resume* offers scope to contrast the simple past and present perfect effectively. Such work would certainly generate numerous utterances such as: *'I studied at university in America/I have lived in Greece for over 3 years.'*

14 Clarify the Conditionals

The conditionals represent something of a mystery to many learners, especially since the various combinations of tenses appear complex. People from other countries must wonder how *'If I won a million dollars…'* can be past tense when apparently talk is of the future. Matters become clearer, however, once the teacher has established that the conditionals have nothing at all to do with time: they are entirely about possibilities, the chances, the odds!

The general conditional, which serves to describe eternal truths, is used for statements that are always true, for example: *If you heat water to 100 degrees Celsius, it boils.* This 100% certainty is conveyed by the simplicity of the tenses, present simple plus present simple. We are dealing with reality.

The first conditional is perhaps well suited to presentation in a context such as holiday planning, sporting contests with two teams, or to the imminent arrival of a new baby girl or boy (if culturally admissible) with dilemmas concerning possible choices of gift. In a travel scenario a family might be discussing whether to go to cool Canada or steamy Bangkok. In this context therefore, utterances such as *'If we go to Canada, we'll take our windcheaters/If we go to Bangkok we'll need our swimming things'* could well occur naturally, the key concept questions being: *Is it quite likely or quite unlikely they will go to Canada? What are the chances of them going to Canada?* The 50/50 answer to the second question defines the first conditional and this move away from certainty or reality is reflected in the differing combination of tenses, i.e. present simple plus 'will' future.

We now revert to the introductory case, the second conditional, with examples such as: *If I won a million dollars, I'd travel round the world* – the example indicating the most common context. Here the relevant concept questions to put to learners are: *Is winning so much money likely or unlikely? Very very unlikely? But is it impossible?* Through such enquiries it can be established that the second conditional is used when events are highly unlikely but not impossible, the chances now being well under 1%. This increased distance from fact and reality is rendered by the simple past plus 'would' conditional tense. Of course in the last two examples the abbreviations 'We'll' and 'I'd' require elucidation.

The complexity of form in third conditional sentences appears daunting. However, presenting these in the context of making excuses soon provides useful examples such as: *If I hadn't missed the bus, I wouldn't have been late/If I had caught the bus. I would have been here on time.* Now the remoteness of the tenses conveys the hypothetical nature of the statements, the chances of altering the real-life situation being nil. This is rightly called *'The too late conditional'*. And – interestingly, where the form is negative – as in the first example – the meaning is positive (I did miss the bus. I was late) and where the form is positive – as in the second example – the meaning is negative (I didn't catch the bus. I was not on time).

15 Provide Plenty of Meaningful Practice

Given the excesses of Behaviourism, practice activities have fallen somewhat into disrepute, yet they may still be necessary if learners are to achieve a reasonable degree of automaticity in their speech. Apart from engaging with elicitation as suggested above, oral proficiency can be enhanced through deliberate practice activities intended to foster the conscious learning of language – pair and group work routines being particularly conducive. Younger learners in particular still retain a good ear for language having recently acquired L1 almost exclusively through exposure and may take readily to such activities, which – in a pre-, while- and post-task format – could occur as required at any stage.

The classroom certainly can represent an authentic setting for purposeful L2 language, but it cannot generate the quantity or perhaps quality of a true immersion situation where the entire environment is permeated by the target language. Practice therefore has its place – the crucial thing being to render any necessary, if rather repetitious, routines meaningful. This is usually done: by insisting that student responses are true; by requiring students to add a reason or similar additional element; or by presenting the language practice in a game-like format. Some examples are provided below by way of illustration.

Flash cards, providing that these convey meaning clearly and unambiguously, offer an effective means of practising new or recently encountered language items. A suitable set for beginners might portray adjectives such as the antonyms *fat/thin, tall/short, rich/poor, old/young, ugly/beautiful, strong/ weak, rich/poor etc.* The pictures can be shown in turn to all learners and the whole item (not just a single word) elicited, for example *'s/he's young'.* This type of fast-paced oral routine can move from whole class to group to individual responses and from repetition through either/or to open questions (i. e. from easier to somewhat more demanding responses) with items being revised in cyclical fashion as the teacher progresses through the set of cards.

A similar set, possibly for a somewhat older class, might have pictures of animals and require learners to express likes and dislikes, being required to say the truth and give a reason. *'I like dogs because they are friendly/I don't like dogs because they are dangerous.'* Such simple routines with their copious practice opportunities promote oral proficiency for all, since cover can be provided by whole class, group and/or pair work before individual responses are required. If the great majority of the class can produce the required language effortlessly from the picture prompts without reading words from the cards (which would be reading practice only), then they are beginning to get hold of some useful language and becoming used to speaking.

Picture cards can also be employed in oral practice games such as *Noughts and Crosses/Bingo.* Games, where individuals or teams compete to win, are highly motivating and disguise the repetitive nature of the language practice. Good games must have an element of chance too, so that all learners stand a chance of winning. In this game nine already well-practised pictures are arranged in three parallel rows of three on one side of the whiteboard, using a non-binding adhesive. A corresponding noughts and crosses grid with nine fields is then drawn on the other side and the class divided into two teams. The teacher then invites one pupil in one team to 'say a card'. In a set concerning common activities s/he might choose to say *'She's playing tennis'* or *'He's reading a book'.*

According to the position of the card chosen, an X is marked in the corresponding slot on the whiteboard grid. Then a pupil from the opposite team is nominated and the procedure repeated with an O marked in the appropriate place. The first team to get a row down, across or diagonally (use gestures) wins. The game is so familiar students need only minimal instructions, perhaps just a short 'trial run'. One game takes a mere 3 minutes and can therefore be repeated a further two times. Sometimes the teacher nominates better pupils first, then good ones in order to provide a model for others. In the final round, pupils who produce a correct utterance could perhaps name a player on the opposition team, this usually ensuring that 'weaker' pupils are called upon to answer – but only after hearing the answers twice already.

As with sport, rules about inappropriate help to team mates or slow responses should mean that the offending team misses a turn. This simple game played three times can allow up to 27 students to speak (not read) individually. As the game proceeds, the teacher should commentate positively on progress, for example *'Good move! Good tactics! Well done!'*

In practice, weaker learners sometimes produce correct language items (they focus on what they know) which are, however, tactically inappropriate and unhelpful for their team. This may cause unintended amusement and/or annoyance to the team and it is then incumbent on the teacher to protect 'face' through some remark such as *'Well it's a good answer. The English is perfect, but it's not really the one you needed.'*

There are innumerable possible practice activities. At an intermediate level the treatment of controversial social issues could involve an Alley Debate where two teams prepare arguments for or against a stated proposition. They then stand in two facing rows with each opposing pair, in turn, having one minute each to state aspects of their team's case. The teacher moves forward as each pair finishes their turn veering slightly towards one side of the alley or the other to indicate who did best. After all pairs have spoken, an overall judgement and evaluation is given. An easier version is the Doughnut Debate with a stationary inner circle of eight and a rotating outer one which poses a given set of questions to each respondent allowing the latter to become ever more adept at answering a series of repeated questions.

16 Don't Forget Dialogues

Dialogues have in the past been over-exploited yet they still retain some advantages. They can offer a realistic, colloquial and/or socially appropriate model of English and incorporate the principle that conversation is usually cooperative. The context can be made explicit so that learners know exactly who is speaking, where they are and why they are talking. And dialogues teach almost everything: vocabulary; grammar; intonation, stress, rhythm; pronunciation; fillers; hesitations; politeness, register and appropriacy.

If the teacher has available or has written a suitable, topic-related dialogue that has a beginning, middle and end and is not distorted by undue structural dominance, two or three pre-listening questions may be set to focus initially on content and meaning. This reduces learner workload since not everything must be memorised, as is sometimes expected. Learners may then answer individually but can be encouraged to consult in pairs to increase cooperation and lessen anxiety. In any case two or three learners speak.

The dialogue, hopefully with contrasting male and female voices and varying interaction patterns (e.g. Q, Q + A), can then be replayed or re-presented with the pre-listening questions this time focusing on some language element, perhaps the form of a particular tense. *'What words does s/he use to....?'* Again two or three students might respond, this time identifying the target item or structure (if any).

The text can then be issued or displayed and practised – chorally with a strong teacher-led model to avoid chanting and flat intonation and/or with the respective roles assigned to male and female groups. Pair work can follow with random feedback ensuring that all learners participate actively, making good use of their speaking time and receiving encouraging and helpful feedback from the teacher. All this results in much speaking, although not all practice options will be used in any one lesson: variation and alternation are required.

Learners can also be encouraged to create 'their own dialogue' through a process of substituting underlined content words (possibly with vocabulary help or scaffolding) or they can be offered a different but similar scenario which permits somewhat greater freedom to produce, practice and present to the class a parallel dialogue. Credit would be given for initiative and originality within the confines of the activity.

Disappearing Dialogue can also be attempted on rare occasion. It must be handled as a game or challenge since it is repetitive. Here – after the class has had a minute to remember the original practised dialogue by looking at the full text displayed via the overhead projector (OHP), visualiser or computer – content words are progressively removed (the easiest first) in a series of 3 further transparencies or slides. Lines of the appropriate length indicate the new gaps and act as a memory prompt. Each new slide or transparency is reprised by the students until, until, by the last one, only the little grammatical words and marked gaps remain. Many students are amazed to discover they can perform a fluent, authentic dialogue from such minimal clues. Again there is much oral practice.

Having covered a dialogue or dialogues in some of the ways outlined above, consideration can be given to a half-dialogue as follow-up homework task. This provides only what one speaker in an exchange says and learners are expected to complete the other part, any appropriate answer being acceptable. This is a good follow-up exercise after an oral lesson, since it builds on and extends the dialogue work already done, involves reading and writing skills and practices inferencing skills that require deeper levels of processing. For example, the utterances of A are left blank with B's responses provided:

A: ....

B: Yes, please. White.

A: ....

B: Sure. Just one spoonful, please.

In this case, the answers might include remarks such as *Tea or coffee?/With sugar or without?* A half-dialogue can also be presented in a circle with 8 or 10 equal segments. Alternate segments are left blank and the half dialogue arranged clockwise in the other spaces. The rubrics ask the learner to decide where the dialogue starts and to provide appropriate utterances in the blank segments.

Other classroom possibilities exist. If the topic is food and drink, there might, for instance, be some role play work offering freer practice. A survey of food and drink preferences would then offer a production activity within given parameters, either conducted in groups or permitting unrestricted classroom movement. In this case a demonstration might be given, survey sheets issued and learners required to question at least 8 other classmates recording their names and tastes. This would be a highly interactive fluency activity where the teacher might well participate but would strive not to interfere (except perhaps when intervening to re-focus and/or lower noise levels). Learners would then report back to the class about specific people, so re-using the necessary language yet again, rather than merely focusing on numbers and statistics.

Eventually such work could involve a task. Following dialogue, role play or survey work (not perhaps cognitively challenging), groups could be assigned to order a meal from the same authentic or semi-authentic menu and to present their order through an acted dialogue between the customers and the waiter/waitress. One set of groups (physically remote from each other in the classroom) might be instructed to place an order for two rich businessmen dining out on an expense account. Another set of groups might need to order for two poor university students, another for two vegetarians and yet another for a romantic couple. In turn the two groups with the same customers could present their solutions/dialogues with consequent discussion concerning who placed the *most appropriate* order and *why* (i.e. focus on meaning). The teacher might – at the end – draw attention to successful language use and to any important linguistic needs that became evident either during the process of learning or in the product dialogues.

Such activities should foster considerable S-Ss interaction and negotiation, both when they choose their respective dishes and drinks and when they evaluate the resulting orders. Such interaction is deemed to foster Second Language Acquisition.

17 Play Vocabulary Games

Given that one main focus of this book is oral proficiency, there is no time to consider what a word is or what is involved in knowing a word. Nor can things such as collocations, connotations or the influence of context on meaning receive attention. Ways of introducing lexical sets can, however, be noted.

Realia (real objects), such as *'carton of, bottle of, can of…'* are motivating and classroom objects can be used to practice prepositions of location. Unambiguous flash or picture cards can convey single actions *('s/he's swimming')*, wall charts can illustrate scenes outside the classroom (e.g. *the beach*), maps can help with country names while teacher drawings can show fine differences in meaning (e.g. *tree/bush*). Miming can convey meaning through action where verbal explanation is difficult (e.g. *stroll, stride, stagger, stumble, swagger*). Scales too can indicate meaning (e.g. *always 100%, usually 80%, often 60%, sometimes 40%, rarely 20%, never 0%*). Expected series (e.g. *red, yellow, green, blue, white…*) also facilitate uptake while arrows can clarify the direction of movement towards or away from the speaker (e.g. *bring/take*).

Lexical relations can also be invoked. Known synonyms (words with similar meanings) may be provided to gloss a new word (e.g. *donate/give*) while antonyms (e.g. *rich/poor*) contrast pairs of opposites. Attention may also be drawn to complementary pairs (e.g. *uncle/aunt, son/daughter*) while hierarchical drawings may illustrate relationships between a superordinate (e.g. *flower*) and its hyponyms or subordinate categories (e.g. *daffodil, rose, carnation...*). Dialogues (as indicated) may teach fillers, exclamations and hesitations incidentally (e.g. *OK, er...well.., really? What a shame! Oh dear*) while definitions can cater for items such as *invention* and *discovery*. Semantic mapping is a useful option following the reading of a story. A grid with the word *'Princess'* at its centre could, for example, offer a framework for the elicitation of the attributes, accessories and lifestyle of such a person. As regards learner strategies, guessing from contextual clues is perhaps the key one when listening or reading.

Certainly where computers are available, these give rich access to illustrative visual support material (although clarity of meaning is more important than artistic merit) and online dictionaries and thesauruses offer limitless scope for independent research. Indeed, young learners can build up their own dictionaries while significant new words can also be added to a class word wall to help create a language rich environment.

Games, of course, offer enjoyable ways of practising recently encountered or re-worked vocabulary. One group game for beginners is Memory. Sets of 16 or 32 picture cards illustrating 8 or 16 pairs of words are prepared. The cards are shuffled and placed face-down on a table or desk. The four players then take turns to turn over two cards, trying to find matching pairs. As they turn over the cards they must say the words correctly. If the two cards match, the player keeps that pair and takes an additional turn. If not, s/he turns the two cards back over leaving them in their same original position on the desk. The player with the most pairs wins. This game usually sparks keen participation and, since it requires a good memory and has a strong element of chance, is likely to turn up unexpected winners. The game can also practice pronunciation too if minimal pair words like ship (short vowel) and sheep (long vowel) are used. It might then be called phonetic pelmanism. Absolutely no written clues are provided.

Silhouettes offer another meaningful vocabulary game for beginners with particular visual impact. The silhouettes are cut from paper and placed one by one on the OHP or visualiser, throwing up a large black outline onto the screen or wall. Each one acts as a prompt. For instance, the silhouette of an activity such as dancing can elicit chunks such as *'She's dancing'* or *'She can dance'* or *'She likes dancing'* as appropriate. Again a vigorous oral routine with questions distributed around the class enables pupils to produce the items orally with no reading or writing.

This game may then be followed by *'What's missing?'* where the class is required to look for 30 seconds at the complete set of 8 or 9 silhouettes already on view and remember what is where. The OHP or visualiser light is then switched off by the teacher who deftly removes one of the items. The projector light is then switched on again and the question put: *What's missing?* In crowded classrooms the teacher must ensure pupils sitting close to the projector do not peep when items are removed! The procedure is repeated, perhaps allowing a few pupils to take the teacher's role.

Having suggested simple routines for younger learners, a game that can only be attempted with upper intermediate or advanced learners is now offered for consideration. This game, called adjective barometer, begins with the teacher writing antonyms such as *happy* and *sad* on the board, one fairly near the top and the other fairly near the bottom. Groups are then given 5 minutes to brainstorm as many related words as possible. In turns students from each group then step forward to add one word at a time to the list on the board. The vital thing is that they write their word in the correct place on the barometer since this act alone serves to define the meaning. For instance, *'elated'* or *'overjoyed'*, *'ecstatic'* and *'euphoric'* should be written above *'happy'* and *'glad'* at the side of it. *'Contented'* might be in the middle while items such as *'miserable'*, *'depressed'*, *'heartbroken'* and *'grief-stricken'* would be placed below *'sad'* with *'unhappy'* at the side. Phrases like *'over the moon'* also count. The group that contributes the most correctly placed words on the barometer wins.

Taken together, the ready availability of vocabulary teaching and learning techniques and the ease of access to internet resources and online games (for example *trolley dash – see http://learnenglishkids.britishcouncil.org/en/fun-with-english/ trolley-dash*) suggest that, even though L1 represents a resource rather than an obstacle, translation of vocabulary items is not often necessary or necessarily judicious.

18 Teach Real Language

The ideas so far propounded, however well intentioned, are not likely to foster oral proficiency if the model of spoken English is inauthentic. It has long been suggested that speech and writing represent different codes and that good models of each are required.

Speech is transient, time-bound and dynamic and often occurs in situations where the audience or interlocutor(s) is/are present. Given its spontaneous nature there is little advanced planning with consequent performance features such as repetition, false starts, hesitations, re-phrasing and circumlocution. Indeed, speech is sometimes categorized as not well-formed, since word and sentence boundaries may be unclear with consequent dysfluency effects. However, given the nature of face-to-face interaction, paralinguistic and/or extra-linguistic clues, such as facial expressions and gestures, may facilitate understanding while intonation and pauses may delineate longer chunks or anticipate grammatical boundaries.

Conversation, perhaps the most common form of spoken discourse, is often informal and colloquial. It is well suited to casual social functions and the expression of opinions and attitudes. The advent of corpora, large searchable computer databases of authentic language, have permitted intriguing (previously hard to conduct) explorations of spoken discourse with attention to features, such as hedging which, in relational exchanges, tones down the force of utterances and mitigates any threat to face *(I guess, it's just that I think that…)*, vagueness which indicates sensitivity to the dangers of sounding unduly authoritative *(that sort of thing, kind of thing, a whatchamcallit)* and approximation which avoids pedantic over-precision *(I'll see you at around 6.30)*. Commonly used language 'chunks' of various sizes are also easily identified, for example: *you know, a lot of, and things like that, all that kind of thing, do you know what I mean?*

Writing, by contrast, displays almost antithetical tendencies being space-bound, static, permanent and more unforgiving. The physical remoteness of the anonymous reader dictates the precise, careful and often more formal construction of text, with easily identifiable component parts such as sentences and paragraphs. Whilst it is clear that speech and writing usually operate as separate and distinct communicative channels and as different media, the distinction between the two is becoming gradually blurred by the immediacy of, for example, email or ICQ (Internet 'chat').

One of the traditional features of the written form was always that it was more considered and reflective, the message being revised before dispatch. However, the spontaneous character of internet exchanges in contemporary communication may strongly reproduce the stylistic effects of the spoken language.

The provision of authentic or at least semi-authentic models of spoken English including awareness of regional and social varieties and perhaps even of *English as a Lingua Franca*, is essential.

19 Beware of the Textbook

Textbooks are an important aid to teaching, although quality varies greatly and selection is not easy. Some teachers prefer to construct their own tailor-made materials, others adapt the chosen or imposed works but many place great reliance on officially sanctioned books. Often regarded as a problem or necessary evil, they may embody an unfortunate compromise between commercial and pedagogical imperatives, sometimes offering little more than neatly presented trash. They can be good servants but should never be permitted to dictate teaching objectives. In colonial or post-colonial settings they may tend to look inward to C1 (the home culture) rather than outwards to the English-speaking world at large. In more monolithic countries they may even propound state ideology.

More worryingly, even so-called revised or up-to-date books may continue to embody a traditional, strongly structural approach to language teaching while purportedly offering a task-based approach. In such a case any shift to current approaches would barely be discernable. In competitive, elite systems, where selection rather than education is paramount, the indiscriminate use of textbooks may even lead to the 'Race Against Time' phenomenon (or 'Hurry Along Curriculum') where concern for testing, accountability and standards may almost oblige teachers knowingly to revert from sound constructivist child-centred practice to outmoded norms in order to satisfy the objectives of the curriculum planners. In such contexts textbooks are not likely to furnish good models of spoken English. Indeed, as seen in the section on methods, their deficiencies are considerable. In a worst case scenario, they might propose dialogues as flawed as this fictitious example:

Father (F) is showing Susan (S) and Peter (P) some old family photos

P: Look, Susan. Father used to be thin. Now he is fat.

F: I was ten then. Now I am sixty.

S: Where was it?

F: It was in a village. I used to live there with my parents. Now I live in Jakarta. I used to live in a small hut but now I live in a flat.

J: The country has changed.

F: Yes, there used to be farms. There used to be fields everywhere. And there used to be cattle in the fields. Now there are only houses and roads.

The issues are obvious: the question of politeness (a cultural variable); the unnatural frequency of the 'then and now' framework and repeated target structure ('used to'); the use of whole sentences; the lack of short forms such as *'He's'*; and fact that shared knowledge is recounted as new (the children might not know how old their father is but they certainly know where he lives – in the Jakarta flat with them!). This is a contrived, artificial model serving only to display target vocabulary items together with the grammatical structure of the day.

20 Prompt Pupil Responses

Apart from simply asking questions, it is also useful to be able to prompt learners by offering helpful hints or clues, especially if learners are hesitant or unable to provide the answers independently. In such cases (assuming of course the questions are not completely beyond the learner's knowledge or capabilities), the teacher can provide scaffolding by offering prompts, possibly through reformulation or re-phrasing, through elaboration of a point made or half-made by a learner, through an alternative question or simply through a request for clarification.

Starting from an initial enquiry, such as *'What can you tell me about the air quality?'*, s/he could then proceed to ask *'Well, how clean do you think the air is in Shanghai? Is it reasonably clean or rather dirty? What do you mean by 'bad'?'* There may also be semantic or syntactic adjustments to the teacher language in order to ensure pupil comprehension – in much the same way as native speakers and care takers adjust their language level to something just beyond the listener's current proficiency level (L+1) when addressing foreigners or young children.

Skill in questioning is, however, of little use if the teacher then completely ignores what the pupils say. Teachers must take an interest in and respond to pupil ideas in an encouraging way, sometimes asking follow-up questions – *'Yes. And why is the air so dirty sometimes? What is it like where you live? Right, so you still go hiking. Who with? Where?'* One of the ways in which teachers promote an on-going dialogue with their students is to take what students say and use it as the basis for what they themselves say next. In this way, the learners' own remarks become part and parcel of the teaching and learning process. The most obvious way of doing this is through confirmation (as, for example, a teacher's *'Yes, that's right'* in response to a learner's answer). Repeating the things learners say is another possibility, one which allows the teacher to focus the attention of the whole class on a student contribution that possesses educational value.

Even where student answers are partly or wholly incorrect there may be some element which can be turned to good effect through further probing: *Yes I agree. Pollution is bad, but do you really think it is caused by a lack of wind?* Teachers can also indicate solidarity with the learners by making *'We statements'* (for example: *Yesterday we were talking about technology and gadgets. Which ones did we say were the best?*). These reveal a commonality of purpose as well as reactivating past experience so rendering this relevant to the activities to come. In this way shared knowledge and collective understanding can promote further progress.

21 Give Learners Thinking Time

It is also important to permit learners some 'wait' or 'thinking time' after a question has been posed rather than expecting an instantaneous response. Indeed, if teachers can be more tolerant of silence there may be beneficial consequences for both the teacher and the learners.

As regards the teachers, there may be: fewer failures to respond; an increase in the length of responses; an increase in unsolicited responses; more S-S discussion; more questions from students; a greater teacher acceptance of a wider variety of responses; and an increase in student oral confidence. Indeed pupils may receive a wider variety of teacher questions and there may be fewer self-answers by the teacher.

As for the teachers, the benefits might include: increased flexibility and continuity in the development of ideas; fewer but more cognitively complex lines of enquiry; more effective incorporation of student responses into the on-going discourse; heightened, more positive expectations of learner contributions, including those from previously 'invisible' individuals. Increased wait time may therefore be generally beneficial in mitigating teacher dominance.

The tendency not to wait for answers may, to some extent, originate not just in teacher's possible unease with silence but also in false or sanitized versions of speech which often edit out or omit the natural pauses, hesitations, false starts and repetitions. These, however, offer time for thought, the redundant or repeated elements often facilitating better comprehension.

22 Do a Reality Check

There are, as noted, many ways in which pupils' contributions may be encouraged: questioning and practice in all its guises; elicitation; pair work; group work; mingle activities; and games. The prevailing methodology (traditional, oral-structural, communicative, task-based) and the purposes of the activities (meaning or form/fluency or accuracy) will largely determine the nature and extent of the classroom interaction.

At the end of a predominantly oral lesson of 40 minutes, students can be asked to indicate by raising their hands if they had answered a question individually during the lesson. (They may, of course, also have engaged with other pupils in pair or group work). If only 10-20% respond, participation is rather low. If 50% are actively engaged that is a good sign. 70% is very good.

This procedure would certainly reveal overall participation rates but, more importantly, would show who was not getting a turn, being unintentionally overlooked or missed out for whatever (probably sub-conscious) reason. The teacher could then be sure to include such disadvantaged individuals in future. The greater the individual participation the more lively, well disciplined and productive the lesson is likely to be.

23 Respond Constructively

Whether responding to oral or written work, the teacher's tone should be positive and helpful: student strengths should be perceived and acknowledged before areas for improvement are considered. With oral work, where learners may feel particularly vulnerable, a warm acceptance of students' willingness to participate is advisable together with tact and discretion in handling offerings that are in some way deficient. Not to say that direct correction is necessarily negative – handled well it provides valuable information about how language does *not* work.

As already noted, errors (where the learner does not know the correct form), mistakes (where the correct form is known but not used) and slips are inevitable given the extensive online mental processing requirements of speech. Teachers might also remember that native speakers are generally tolerant of error, dis-preferring direct correction unless communication is impaired. Learners can therefore often be given opportunities for self- or peer correction.

With writing, it would be hoped that thorough preparation, drafting and editing would produce scripts of reasonable quality. Here again it is vital to respond first to meaning when reading and assessing pupil scripts. If the students have written an essay or story of some sort, the teacher can respond to particular points or highlights in a personal way, for example: *'Yes. I agree legal protection is essential for migrant workers/*

61

Poor Annie. She must have felt terrible when she dropped the Cup.'

Positive comments can also be made on form. Writing about a picnic a student might produce the following stretch of direct speech: *A goat has eaten our sandwiches and it's too wet to light a fire and cook something. I'm cold, wet and hungry. I'm going home!* This can be highly commended for its natural, authentic style which captures the rhythm and cadences of spontaneous speech. Students may also express fine shades of meaning, for instance: *We all laughed at her and she also laughed herself.* Such instances can be explicitly praised.

Teachers can also identify appropriate discourse features in the writing, such as verb harmony, noting the consistent use of the simple past in a narrative. Well placed ticks are encouraging too. When marking student work, teachers can consider whether they will identify every single error (pressure from school authorities and/or parents and students can lead to unfortunate over-correction) or mainly target ones, whether the teacher will mark in pencil (less threatening) or pen, whether there will be differentiation between major and minor mistakes through colour coding, and whether a correction code will be used. Teachers can also restrain an instinct to cross out or underline heavily, perhaps using dotted lines or brackets for minor stylistic adjustments.

Apart from the more technocratic aspects, other key decisions must be made: will the student writing be done by hand (to practice for examinations) or through the use of a word processing programme that facilitates drafting and revision; who will undertake the majority of corrections (hopefully the student); is time spent analyzing or correcting work productive or would further exposure to English be better; and, will teaching opportunities to help the learner be seized?

One way to reduce depressing error is to engage in performance analysis. This would identify cases where the learner made a series of almost identical errors, grouping these in a column under the script (for example: *We were looked, we were saw, we were went*) with correct instances of the use of the simple past by the same writer displayed in an adjacent column *(We went, we ate, we bought)*. It could then be pointed out that by grasping one single point, several errors could be instantly eradicated and the overall impression vastly improved.

Again, where learners confuse or conflate different expressions as with *'she didn't hurt'* – these can be teased apart to provide *'she wasn't hurt/she didn't hurt herself'*. These are teaching opportunities. In general, whether responding to oral or written work, specific, constructive comment that aids learning is better than negative assumptions of carelessness or lack of effort.

24 Praise Good Work

Giving praise is another possible way of offering encouragement. It should be noted, however, that cultural attitudes towards praise vary considerably. It is reported, for instance, that Chinese teachers and parents tend to give less praise than their Western counterparts. Indeed, Chinese mothers are reputedly very hard to please, sometimes expressing dissatisfaction with high or even very high levels of academic achievement. Such demanding behaviour is thought to avoid spoiling the child and to encourage ever greater diligence and studious application. Given a competitive educational ethos and a long-term need to provide financial security for elderly family members, such pressure may secure certain economic advantages through increased upward social mobility.

To outsiders, this approach may appear negative and harsh. Western parents and teachers tend to be more lavish in their praise. In this case, however, Chinese observers may consider the praise to be given randomly and with little justification so that it becomes almost meaningless. Since there is no 'correct' or agreed praise procedure, a middle way may be best. Praise would be given fairly generously but for good reason. It should be justified or deserved praise given for some specific student action, not just tossed around at random.

The comment might be a short one of a formulaic type like *'Well done'* or *'Good job'*. But it could also take the form of a full praise statement that spells out in some detail exactly what it is that the learner has done well. For example, the teacher might say: *I like the use of vocabulary here. Words like 'calm' and 'peaceful' give the reader a sense of the atmosphere as the sun sets.* Such full praise statements are very effective.

25 Manage the Classroom Effectively

Managing active oral participation from students depends on understanding the roles of the teacher at different stages of the lesson. Most teachers are confident during the initial teacher-led phases of lesson where new topics and new language are presented. They may, however, become more hesitant when handling student-centred free practice and production activities or tasks.

There are several possible reasons. In some settings the school culture may emphasise silence and obedience so that even on-task, busy noise and particularly pupil movement are seen as a potentially unwelcome threat to order and as a potential disruption to other classes. And teachers and pupils may simply be more accustomed to a teacher-centred, transmissive style of instruction. In consequence, teachers may appear happy when presenting material themselves (even with Principals prowling the school corridors to detect noise) but they may quickly allow things to drift out of control when conducting less familiar practice and production activities. In such circumstances, learners are often not slow to sense teacher unease and can then 'play up', talking in L1 and making 'naughty' or 'off-task noise'. In such cases, teachers may then blame 'modern methods' for causing chaos.

One vital point to grasp therefore is that pupil-centred activity requires much stronger, more effective but friendly and democratic management, not less. The teacher is now the facilitator (manager) who organizes and runs the activities, not the presenter. If learner-centred oral activities are fairly new and unfamiliar, it is important to remember that change takes time. It is probably best to start small and advance slowly since new routines need to be taught and learnt.

One facet of classroom management is the delivery of clear instructions that tell pupils what to do and how to do it. KISS (keep it short and simple) is a useful acronym, since instructions are best kept simple, specific and precise with delivery at the right place. For instance, the required action should be clearly stated. For example: *Work in pairs (2); Work in groups (3+); Take turns to… .* Specify who does what: *You ask first. Then you answer.* Set specific and realistic time limits: *You have three minutes. Work hard.* And indicate clearly that you will take feedback later: *I'm going to listen to several pairs doing the role play in a few minutes. Be ready.*

Instructions (and explanations) should be well sequenced with appropriate signaling words, such as *first, then, next, finally.* The instructions should be given clearly, neither too quickly nor too slowly, with natural rhythm, stress and intonation patterns and supported by visual and paralinguistic aids, such as pictures and gestures.

Most importantly, a teacher-student or better still a student-student demonstration should be given so learners can see and hear what to do and realise it is not at all difficult. Check comprehension too not by saying *'Do you understand?'* but by asking *'What do you do first, then, next…?'*

26 Maintain cooperation

Given the possible cultural factors discussed earlier, it is unlikely that learners will always appreciate the value of oral work. Games, for instance, may be dismissed as trivial since their very real and serious language learning purposes often remain unstated.

In some settings therefore the learning agenda needs to be made overt through explicit justifications. Indeed, learners might be helped to grasp the value of pair and group work by calculating the speaking time that would be available to each individual in a class of 40 pupils during a 35 minute lesson if the teacher were to stay silent and turns were equally distributed – less than a minute a person. They may then appreciate that pair and group work are essential in providing student speaking time, perhaps 5 to 10 minutes per lesson. It bears repeating that you learn to speak by speaking – not by writing.

This kind of insight may encourage more students to participate. Most students, especially those confined within restrictive systems, quite naturally love variety and often become extremely excited at the prospect of any new game or game-like activity. Teachers therefore need to anticipate this natural reaction. They should provide clear instructions and clear rules for games. For instance, pupils calling out loudly at the wrong time or whispering the answers to friends are told to miss a go. Pupils who hesitate unduly (so destroying the pace of the activity) are simply counted out and their turn offered to their opponents.

As in sport, the rules must be followed. It is inevitable that noise levels will rise after a few minutes with genuinely interactive games and with tasks. Teachers should therefore expect to intervene, clapping their hands for attention, awaiting silence, re-emphasising the purpose and urgency of the task and then re-starting it with a gentle reminder that noise levels must be contained. Some teachers appoint group work 'noise monitors'.

Perhaps the most essential factor in sustaining oral work is to promote accountability. Written work is usually marked, so a somewhat similar regime is required for oral work: after every oral activity there should a public performance by learners. Instructions, such as *'Now you have four minutes to practise. Be busy. I'm going to listen to some of your dialogues at the end'* can concentrate minds and reduce the use of L1. When time is up, 2 or 3 randomly selected pairs or groups must perform for the class. This provides both added speaking and listening practice and an opportunity for greater encouragement. It also acts as a disciplinary control since pupils come to realise that any lack of practice on their part is very likely to be spotted, commented on and noted.

Consistently monitoring learner performance quickly eliminates problems of control and reinforces the high value placed on oral activities. A golden rule might be: *After every oral activity always have learner feedback.*

27 Engage with Children's Literature

Having examined the direct provision of speaking opportunities and associated management issues, other avenues to oracy can be considered. Shared Reading, for instance, necessarily entails much speaking for younger learners. Good children's literature has permanence: it can withstand the test of time and captivate children of different generations. Its special or unique characteristics exert a strong personal appeal, possessing the power to connect with a reader and the reader's experiences, imagination, attitudes or feelings.

Listening to and sharing real books with an adult in the classroom owes much to the Western tradition of the 'bedtime story': it is designed to provide an intimate bonding experience through engagement with and immersion in whole texts in an authentic, meaningful and print-rich classroom context. Children's literature is entirely different from the usual school textbooks since the focus is almost exclusively on meaning. This facilitates a natural integration of skills.

Coursebooks	Children's Literature
intended for grammar and vocabulary teaching;	designed to delight;
predictable contexts, i.e. situational dialogues;	contexts are rich and varied; *continued overleaf ...*

language and situations are often unnatural, contrived and unrepresentative of authentic language, spoken or written;	contains characters, settings, themes and events that are highly interesting, imaginative and entertaining;
contain short isolated sentences that display target grammatical structures;	the language used to portray events and characters is richer, intrinsically more interesting, more inspired and inventive;
children laboriously learn language by completing dull exercises and drills, and answering low level comprehension questions.	children acquire whole chunks of language in context without conscious effort by listening to, reading aloud and responding orally to real texts.

Children's literature is therefore often the foundation for a lifelong love of reading. It provides an inherently interesting, rich and meaningful context for later explicit instruction in and modeling of reading skills and strategies and specifically for the development of phonological, syntactic, semantic and pragmatic awareness. It is therefore important for the teacher to share real books with the learners and to guide them onwards to independent book choices and independent reading.

28 Bring out the Big Books

Big Books are enlarged versions of children's storybooks for young learners. They have a small amount of text on each page with words that are large enough to be seen by a group or class of pupils gathered close to the teacher. They repeat (often in a parallel sequence of three) large chunks of language so permitting readers to predict what will be found when the page is turned. At the same time the language has a natural cadence or rhythm that facilitates reading aloud while relevant, large, interesting and attractive illustrations support the construction of meaning.

Such Big Books give the learners an initial understanding of what it means to be a reader in L2 and provide a springboard for oral and written responses through post-reading activities such as role-play, painting, drawing, and writing. They are not difficult to use as there is a basic five step procedure.

First the class is required to sit close to the teacher who places the book on a stand so that it is clearly visible to everyone. The teacher usually sits at the side. Secondly, the teacher draws attention to the book cover and asks a number of related questions about the title and illustrations intended to arouse interest and curiosity and possibly to draw on previous congruent knowledge or previous reading experiences. Key vocabulary items may also be introduced (for example by taking realia out of a bag) but often their meaning is self-evident in the context of the narrative and care must be taken not to give away the storyline. Learners may at this point predict what may happen in the story, suggestions being noted on the whiteboard. Thirdly, the teacher reads the story aloud bringing it to life through appropriate intonation, facial expressions and associated gestures. Short, incidental comments may draw attention to interesting detail but questioning will be limited since it is vital not to destroy the sense of story.

Occasionally, at the end of a page, learners might make informed guesses about what might happen next. At the end of the book predictions made at the start can be checked and positive comment given. The second reading forms the fourth stage of the procedure and requires the children to join in actively, but with the teacher still leading in order to ensure good pronunciation, stress, rhythm and intonation. Young learners may respond in a variety of ways – some may read along with the teacher, some may produce only the repeated patterned language while others may just follow the pictures and listen.

To maximize participation the teacher may pause before patterned words or phrases and let children supply the missing words. At the end of the second reading the learners should offer a personal response to the story, sharing verbally their feelings and ideas about characters, events and illustrations. After engaging in shared reading, follow-up tasks can provide explicit instruction in reading skills and strategies and/or generate speaking and writing opportunities. This represents the final or fifth stage.

Where available, electronic storybooks with their multimedia combination of sound and image offer learners computer-based interaction with the text through features such as interactive speech bubbles, clickable hot spots and the like.

29 Map out the Follow-up

Having read the story, it is important to follow up enthusiastically. One of the most valuable possibilities is a story map where an elicitation process can allow the discourse structure of the narrative genre to be displayed visually on the whiteboard, the title/author being at the centre of the map with key aspects radiating off.

Questions would therefore relate to the characters (usually people or animals), to the setting (perhaps a castle, forest or city), to the plot (the events that happen), to some problem, complication or conflict that arises and to a solution, resolution or climax where the issue is finally resolved. There may also be a moral or coda to the story, either implicit or explicit, which can be drawn out and discussed. Difficult words such as characters (who?) and setting (where?) would be glossed.

Another follow-up activity that promotes oral work is Readers' Theatre, which is an oral interpretation of a piece of literature read in a dramatic style with readers bringing characters to life through their voices or gestures. A story, a poem, a scene from a play, even a song lyric can provide the ingredients for the script. Readers' Theatre helps children understand and appreciate the richness of language, the ways in which to interpret the language and how language can be a powerful means for the comprehension and appreciation of different forms of literature. Since there may be little action and few props (perhaps only headbands), the reader's voice must convey the feelings, the ideas, and attitudes of the characters through good voice projection, intonation, inflection, and pronunciation skills. All this allows the integration of language arts activities, such as reading the story, creating the script, preparing some necessary props and participating actively (usually in groups), in the interpretation and delivery of the story. It also strengthens the development of critical thinking, creativity and cooperation.

The children may also be asked to perform a role play that mirrors events at an interesting juncture in the story or they could prepare and present a scaffolded and rehearsed radio or TV interview with one or more of the main story characters. Learners might also be asked to produce, illustrate and present an imaginary diary entry for a leading character. These are purposeful and life-like activities. There are, of course, innumerable perhaps more pedestrian possibilities, such as correcting facts, sequencing, crosswords, character report cards, book reviews or even the generation of a parallel small book (one or at most two short pages per learner only since writing is slow).

Generally speaking, teachers who operate in fairly traditional settings are often greatly surprised both by the quantity but also the quality of young children's utterances which may exceed expectations in untold ways. Unfortunately, however, they may cite the need to cover (not uncover) a packed test and examination oriented curriculum as a deterrent to innovation. Informational books on topics such as houses, cars or the weather are, of course, equally vital to learner development and are read avidly.

30 Tune into Music

Music is an international language with even greater appeal than English. Exploited well, rhymes, jazz chants, limericks and songs can generate much active oral work and give learners a real 'feel' for English. Indeed, the affective, motivational and linguistic advantages of such activities are too numerous to mention, but include inclusivity, confidence, rapport, movement, enjoyment and contextualized learning. For every age group and every topic there is probably a suitable item. For young learners, traditional and/or teacher composed rhymes and chants generate positive 'vibes' and provide opportunities to savour the rhythms or heartbeat of English. Indeed, the sample rhymes below can be sung and mimed by the class. It is great fun and compendiums of such items are readily available.

Miss Polly had a dolly	
Miss Polly had a dolly,	He looked at Miss Polly,
Who was sick, sick, sick,	And he shook his head,
So she called for the doctor,	And he said to Miss Polly,
To come quick, quick, quick,	Put her straight to bed,
The doctor came with his bag and his hat.	He took out a pad and he wrote out a pill,
And he knocked on the door, With a tat-tat-tat-tat-tat.	I'll be back in the morning for my bill, bill, bill

I'm a little teapot
I'm a little teapot, short and stout,
Here's my handle,
Here's my spout,
When the water's boiling,
Hear me shout,
Tip me up and pour me out!

Unlike traditional rhymes, Jazz Chants are deliberately written to link the drum beat rhythm of English to the tempo of jazz music. They usually have a teacher solo/whole class chorus format. While they may unconsciously reinforce grammar and vocabulary, their great strength concerns the phonological features of natural speech.

In a four beat line, which learners can clap and tap, only the words *one, two, three, four* may be chanted. Yet, in one well known chant by Christine Graham, the very next ten word line fits the very same four beats: *What's she going to buy at the grocery store?* Here the strongly stressed content words are pronounced in full while the unstressed grammatical ones are reduced to weak forms. The most frequent English vowel *schwa* is therefore much practised as in subsequent phrases such as 'a /ə/ bottle of /əv/ milk'.

Limericks, which hail from the Irish town of the same name, are great fun, although sometimes the humour can be too ribald (teachers beware!). Limericks are five line verses with the rhyme pattern A A B B A that can be sung. It is not hard to make up your own:

There was a young lady named Austin,
Who once bought a dress she got lost in,
She said "This ain't right,
I'll get one that's tight"
So she did but she had to be forced in!

There was a young fellow called Phil,
Who swallowed an atomic pill.
He blew up one night,
And gave us a fright,
So we're looking for bits of him still!

Songs, however, are the gold standard, authentic and hugely motivating, offering engagement and aesthetic pleasure. The choice of song is yours! Treatment, however, should not be restricted to 'listen and fill in the gap' type exercises. Songs, like poems, often have a deeper meaning that needs to be interpreted and responded to in a personal way. Even older songs like Simon and Garfunkel's *El Condor Pasa* retain an appeal for teens and 'tweens. Here learners might be asked to listen a first time and provide words to: describe the sound of the song; identify the instruments they hear; and consider its country of origin.

Rare words such as *'wistful'* might be added and explained and clues in the title exploited. The real-life status and powerlessness of the singer, conveyed through the relationships between simple words such as 'sparrow/*snail*, hammer/*nail*', positions him as perhaps only a peasant farmer or bonded labourer toiling away in the fields and burdened by family or perhaps financial obligations and unable to emulate either the graceful swan who flies free or the condor who soars magnificently high above the mountains.

Indeed, the beauty of the refrain contrasts sharply with the sadness of the lyrics while use of the second conditional makes clear how unlikely it is that this dream of freedom will come to fruition. The language is simple but the message is profound.

I'd rather be a sparrow than a snail,

Yes, I would, if I only could, I surely would.

I'd rather be a hammer than a nail,

Yes, I would, if I only could, I surely would.

Away, I'd rather sail away, like a swan.

That's here and gone,

A man gets tied up to the ground,

he gives the world its saddest sound, its saddest sound….

In a similar way songs like John Lennon's *Imagine*, with its atmospheric *YouTube* video, raise issues of conflict, religion, nationalism, brotherhood and idealism that invite thought and discussion.

In many settings around the world, there may be a dearth of songs in English about the local town or country. The teacher can compose some to tie in with themes such as tourism, transport, food, lifestyle and the like as the few selected verses below indicate. Follow-ups might involve the production and presentation of a collage to encourage tourism and/or a survey of teacher–student opinions on likes and dislikes about school. Reactions to such songs are usually positive.

Here are two Hong Kong songs.

Tourists	
Hong Kong is the City of Light	Some folks go up to the Peak
Its harbour skyline shines so bright	Some stay in restaurants for a week
The Star Ferry gives such cheap rides	Some just eat in dai pai dongs*
To talkative tourists packed inside	Where in the world can beat HONG KONG?
(first verse)	(last verse)
	*open air food stalls

Hurry, Hurry, Hong Kong
Flyovers, fly-unders, skyscrapers, tunnels, just amazing, it's Hong Kong
Carriageways, by-ways, super highways, airport runways, it's Hong Kong
Buses, taxis, cars and lorries, trams and trolleys, it's Hong Kong
KMB, CMB, KCR, MTR, rush hour, crush hour, that's Hong Kong!

You can even sing about the life of a teacher!

Teachers
Meetings and meetings
Marking all night
Grades and percentages
Reports to write
Curriculum
Syllabus
Schemes of work too
All kinds of everything remind me of school!

Songs can also stimulate imaginative and creative responses. For instance, highly personal reactions to a particular piece of modern music can be elicited. Would the student listeners buy it, have it as background or simply turn it off? What do they picture if listening with eyes closed? Can they describe the sort of person who might like or dislike such music (avoiding stereotypes)? What product might this music promote if used in an advertisement? What theme might a film with this music have and/or what might be happening when such music occurs in a film? Would it be a thriller, a romance, a children's film and would it end happily?

Groups of students could also be allocated a short piece of music and asked to create their own advertisement in a way that combines sound, image and language, paying particularly attention to catchy commercial tag lines and their linguistic features. Innovative and original music videos could also be explored, critically analysed and discussed. With upper intermediate and advanced classes such activities permit more or less unfettered language use focused on meaning and fluency. Music is magic!

31 Cash in on Popular Culture

Popular culture is by definition ubiquitous. It is an everywhere, everyday, ever-changing part of mainstream identity and consciousness. Current, fluid and generational, it touches – if not envelopes – students' lives being a likely source of interest and fascination. It is what we eat, what we wear, what we buy, what we watch, listen to and play, what we read and how we interact: fast food; fashion and beauty; brand name products; TV, film and music; comics and cartoons; iPhones, email, Facebook, Twitter and the like. It creates celebrities for the mass audience.

Heavily youth oriented, it offers a world of instantaneous touch-of-the-button interpersonal communication and sharing involving informal language learning, translingual communication, and multimodal dialogue about languages and cultures. In many countries, technological goods previously considered expensive luxuries are rapidly becoming must-haves, a basic pre-requisite for participation in the global village. All this suggests teaching and learning resources as infinite, authentic and appealing as the internet itself.

But although the potential is almost unlimited, some degree of critical media awareness rather than unthinking acceptance is imperative. Consumerism and globalisation often serve the interests of big businesses and corporations with 'cool hunters' constantly seeking to identify and generate new and profitable trends. Media literacy is therefore needed to offer learners the chance to judge for themselves the true merits of a product as they seek to discover and question elements of their own identities, preferences and subjectivities that are perhaps almost created for them by a complex multi-media environment. Key questions might be: *'Who created the message; what attention-getting techniques are used; what is the intended audience and how might people understand the message in the same or differing ways; what lifestyles, cultural and moral values and opinions are conveyed or omitted from the message; and why was this message sent?'*

Advertisements would be a good subject of study given their clever combination of image, sound and text and persuasive or manipulative purposes. The strategies they employ (e.g. emotional associations, humour) and their linguistic features (e.g. catch-phrases, jingles) can certainly be talked about.

Indeed, whatever the text, it is vital to adopt a discourse perspective. For instance, if working on newspapers, perhaps contrasting the popular and serious press, some attention could perhaps be devoted to photo captions. These often have a one-sentence description indicating who or what is being pictured, what are they doing and where they are. Language features include: appositives which provide key information regarding the subject's significance through defining words, phrases or synonyms; the frequent use of the present simple tense in the active voice; and the use of prepositions of place to state the location. The result might be: *'XYZ, famous movie star, opens a new ice skating rink in Rio'*.

Similarly, if the students were producing a movie review they might need to consider and describe: the movie genre (e.g. romantic comedy, thriller); the main plot minus the ending; the main performers and the director; any age restrictions; where the movie is playing; and a star rating system to encourage or dissuade potential viewers. They might add a personal commentary on whether the movie is worth seeing. Attention might be given to: technical vocabulary (e.g. *sequel, comedy, twist*); descriptive adjectives and adverbs (e.g. *scary, violent, exciting*); commonly used phrases and clauses (e.g. *a must-see, a nail-biter, a tear-jerker, a feel-good movie, I would strongly recommend…*); the use of the present tense and of imperatives (e.g. *the films starts with images of… , don't waste your hard earned cash*); and the informality of comment (*I hated this movie/you will just love the scene where…*). For ensuing poster creation and presentation learners might need to identify a striking image that encapsulates the film's very essence.

The strong discourse element evident above can also be appreciated with a topic such as food. Here there might be coverage of narrative texts (e.g. such as stories, songs and poems), persuasive texts (such as posters or advertisements), procedural texts (such as recipes), informational texts (such as shopping lists, coupons, signs and menus) and exchanges (such as cafe conversations or phone calls to order home delivery).

Alternatively such activities can be approached from a multi-skills perspective. A unit on Friendship might well involve listening to video extracts from films such as *Shrek* or *Finding Nemo*, talking about the relationships between humans and animals (as in *Babe*), singing *'You've got a friend in me'* from *Toy Story* or contemplating what life would be like without friends – as in *The Grinch*. Reading might cover commercial greeting cards, suitable narrative texts and/or children's blogs while writing could involve e-cards, an acrostic poem about a best friend and/or pencil portraits and descriptions. Speaking might involve discussing the advantages of Skype or talking about sites like Flickr or Facebook (with a consideration of netlingo and the erosion of boundaries between speech and writing) and/or a mingle find-your-partner matchmaking game with cards giving details of appearance, personality, likes, dislikes and interests.

The possibilities are endless and foster not only language skills but also generic ones, such as collaboration, communication, creativity, critical thinking and IT competency. Short, well selected *YouTube* clips can also have a huge visual and emotional impact in the classroom, conveying a sense of immediacy and originality since they sometimes capture events and happenings beyond the normal public purview. Choices are highly personal but can motivate, for instance through humour (*Sumsing Turbo 3000 XI Multitask; German Coastguard trainee*), action-packed cooking sequences (*Pancakes II Pancakes for your face*) or teenage comment (*Kevjumba*). For digital natives, i.e those born into the digital age, recourse to such resources is almost second nature.

32 Help with Pronunciation

It is not necessary for L2 learners to sound like native speakers, especially given the many varieties of English. Nor is it advisable to conduct pronunciation lessons *per se*. Rather matters of pronunciation should be dealt with as they arise, with a special focus on areas of difference between L1 and L2. The objective is to be readily intelligible so that communication functions well.

There are many aspects to attend to, one being the individual sounds – the vowels and consonants. In this case it is vital that learners actually hear the difference between closely related sounds, so sound discrimination games such as *Odd one out* employing minimal pairs such as *flight/fright* or *slip/sleep* are useful. These words are said by the teacher in a series of four where three words are the same and one different. Learners must identify which one – the first, second, third or fourth – was the odd one out. Consonant clusters such as /bl/ in *black* are also problematic, yet once perceived aurally the sounds become easier to produce. Tongue twisters too are a fun way of practising, as with *Peter Piper picked a peck of pickled peppers*. Fine differences such as the aspiration in *pin* and non-aspiration in *spin* can also be demonstrated with a thin piece of paper held in front of the mouth which moves in the first case with the release of air for the plosive /p/, but not in the second. Websites also offer animations of problematic sounds such as 'th' that show the positions of lips, tongue and teeth.

Since English is a stress-timed (not syllable-timed) language, stress is an important area, both at the word and sentence level, and is strongly associated with the rhythm of speech. Indeed, faulty stress may hinder communication far more than grammatical incorrectness. Stress at the word level is invariable, for example 'forGET' is considered correct but 'FORget' is not. And, if the stress of 'PREsent' is shifted to the second syllable as in 'preSENT', the grammatical function changes from noun to verb. As we know from the treatment of children's rhymes and Jazz Chants, English has – in connected speech – a strong drumbeat rhythm, where content words which carry important information (nouns, main verbs, adjectives and adverbs) are stressed and functional or grammatical words (auxiliaries, articles, prepositions and pronouns) are reduced to weak forms – for example: *'The GIRLS are in the PARK'.*

Sentence stress, however, is more flexible than word stress. Sometimes a speaker may choose to highlight a particular word or phrase to attract the listener's attention. 'I was a TEAcher', for example, has a different emphasis from 'I WAS a TEAcher', the stressed 'WAS' in the second case helping to convey an aspect of the message that might otherwise be missed – s/he has changed job or retired. Contextual factors also exert an influence since new information is stressed whereas old information is not. Dialogues are useful here to make and then practise the point with party or cafe utterances such as: A: 'I think I'll have a tomato *sandwich*.' B: 'And I'll have a *cheese* sandwich.' C: 'A cheese *roll* for me'.

Clapping and tapping offer another way to reinforce rhythm since groups of words with the same number of syllables and same stress patterns can be chanted chorally or in groups. Here is a small selection of possibilities.

I HOPE to, he SAW me, she WENT there, I GUESS so, we'd LOVE to

WATCH him RUN, LET her GO, PUT it HERE, PICK it UP, TAKE it AWAY

The MAN in the MOON, on TOP of the HILL, the WORST of them ALL, they SAID they would GO

How NICE of you, I TOLD you so, he WANTS me to, they've TAKen it

Intonation, which concerns the rise and fall of the voice to various levels as people speak, is also important for meaning. Its different patterns serve a number of functions and indicate the speaker's attitude to his/her interlocutor and/or subject matter.

The falling tone, for instance, suggests certainty on the part of the speaker, a belief in the validity of his/her utterance and conveys an air of finality about what has been said. This indicates a certain degree of speaker dominance: the speaker knows, tells or demands. The matter at hand is closed or complete. The rising tone, by contrast, suggests that the situation is uncertain and still open to negotiation, that there is more to follow. This may indicate speaker-deference: the speaker does not know, is not an authority and is asking or requesting in order to encourage a response. So 'SHUT the door' uttered with falling intonation would represent a demand or order spoken with authority whereas the same words conveyed with rising intonation would convey uncertainty and a request for clarification.

There are other possibilities as with: *A: 'It's a really good school.' B: 'Yes'.* A falling tone on *yes* would indicate agreement to a common sense proposition whereas a fall-rise tone on *yes* would indicate only limited agreement, a certain sense of reservation or doubt which invites reappraisal from the first speaker. In another case a fall-rise pattern might suggest surprise or astonishment. For example: *'You won aGAIN?'* (rise-fall).

Happy Landings Airways

Thank you.
Goodbye.
Enjoy your fright.

Huh?!

/ f r / or / f l / ?

Intonation also has a grammatical function that can correlate to the functions above. Statements of fact have a falling tone, for example: *'He's not coming'*. Wh-questions, such as *'What do you want?'* also have falling intonation whereas open questions, such as *'Do you like the blue one?'* have rising intonation since the enquiry is genuine.

The best thing for teachers to do is to mark the intonation by arrows above the text at the right places in the utterances. Attention can also be drawn to similar range of intonation patterns in tag questions. And lists have a combination of patterns, the final item being spoken with falling intonation to signal the final item, while the preceding items are spoken with rising intonation to let the listener know there is more to follow:

'I need onions, tomatoes, green peppers, and mushrooms.'

33 Treasure the Intangibles

Parents, naturally enough, wish their children to do well in examinations and teachers have a professional obligation to help them achieve the best possible results. Examinations appear, at least on the surface, to be meritocratic and to provide focus and motivation for learning. However, they are not universally acclaimed. Drawing on authorities such as Shohamy, Bourdieu and Tollefson, I once wrote (rather effusively):

High-stakes tests represent a ubiquitous if far from innocuous feature of educational systems the world over. Notorious for creating the illusion of being cost-effective policy making devices, they can allow powerful élites to manipulate educational systems in covert, unchallenged and often unmonitored ways through the imposition of essentially self-serving agendas whose main purpose is to consolidate the continued symbolic domination of the establishment.

Such instruments permit authority to redefine, limit, control and reward that knowledge recognized as socially legitimate, i.e. their own. Tests may consequently be employed as a disciplinary tool to create fear, anxiety and subversion in test takers, coercing candidates into compliance with official demands, distorting the learning process and generating profoundly detrimental effects for the rejected or excluded individual. Tests represent three sources of power: state power (in terms of bureaucracy), discourse power (as tests are imposed on unequal individuals), and ideological power (about what knowledge is worthwhile).

Yet although such uses of tests may be criticised as inherently unethical and undemocratic, an unstated, largely unconscious social compact between those who dominate and those suppressed satisfies a mutual need for the maintenance of discipline, order and hierarchy. The collusion of society at large is thus assured, a degree of acceptance, trust and even faith in such dubious procedures often emerging. The situation becomes yet more complex when colonial and post-colonial language policy issues intrude.

Whatever the merits of those arguments, ever stronger government demands for business-style accountability from both schools and teachers have increased the pressures exponentially. Examinations, which can devour whole years in a student's school career, remain therefore an incontrovertible fact of life, the success or otherwise of a school in examinations often determining both its own status and that of its teachers.

In a worst case scenario, examinations may come to dominate the lives of both teachers and learners resulting in an ethos of relentless testing. In senior school, the demands of impending 'barrier' or 'exclusion' examinations may tempt teachers merely to elucidate the intricacies of endless (rather dry) past papers, spoon-feeding the answers rather than challenging learners to think and contribute. In the middle and lower years, this approach may be reflected in the persistence of the traditional, high pressure, weekly dictation whose traditional format remains inviolable. No new techniques (such as *running dictation, miming dictation* or *mutual dictation*) must intrude since the true purpose is to accumulate scores for rank ordering and the calculation of class positions. At the same time, homework may extend the school day deep into the evening hours while private tuition and extra classes erode the weekends and holidays. The dread grip of examinations can even extend to Kindergartens with tiny tots being required to perform well in order to gain admittance to 'prestige' institutions. This looks like 'exam hell'.

In a best case scenario, the number and frequency of internal end-of-term and end-of-year school examinations would be restricted to a necessary minimum and the time saved devoted to improving the quality of teaching and learning. Interesting, topical and possibly controversial current topics and issues might be addressed in innovative, language-rich ways. Moreover, by shifting the focus from summative assessment (involving assessment *of* learning) to formative assessment (assessment *for* learning), greater attention could be afforded to the value of work done in the classroom, for instance oral presentations, projects, portfolios and the like. Such a teaching – learning – assessment cycle could offer useful feedback to both teachers and learners as they seek success.

Most importantly, straightforward principles of testing (if tests there must be) can be applied in internal school examinations. First, the test should be on the work covered. Secondly, it should be in a familiar format with known question types. *Thirdly, it should be set at the ability level appropriate for the class!* The test can still target validity (measuring what it sets out to measure) and reliability (generating consistent results across parallel groups). Assuming the teachers are normal (they work hard and teach to the best of their ability) and that the learners are normal (they want to learn), the outcomes should then be positively-skewed and far more encouraging. After all, repeatedly experienced success is the motor of continued progress. In this way, we might return from 'Dead-ucation' to Education!

Perhaps therefore we should not overvalue the tangible aspects, i.e. the things that can be measured, and neglect the inner substance. This is particularly true in the case of language teachers, who deal in the global currency of intercultural communicative competence. We should cherish the intangibles: the imperatives of tolerance, compassion, kindness and friendships worth so much more than grades, percentages and bits of paper. We should strive to embody some sort of ethical dimension in teaching, not in a spirit of self-righteousness but in order to recognise, value and confirm the uniqueness of others and to place wisdom above knowledge. We should therefore not make an idol of education but rather reflect the reality of existence beyond, allowing children and young people to get to know the natural world, to climb trees, ride bikes, go fishing, kick a ball around and enjoy friendships. As the great writer Mark Twain once said, *"I never let my schooling interfere with my education"*. So – my best tip? Don't Work Too Hard!

Related
Reading

Since this book is not in a standard academic format, it has not been referenced in the usual way. Through this brief, indicative list I would like to acknowledge the many named (and other) authors who have influenced my thinking. I hope readers may look at some of the titles listed.

I would also like to express my gratitude to the in-service teachers whose ideas are also reflected in the book.

Biggs, J. B. (ed.) (1996) *Testing: To Educate Or To Select.* Hong Kong: Hong Kong Educational Publishing Co.

Bloom, B. S. (1956) *Taxonomy of Educational Objectives: The Classification of Educational Goals. Handbook 1: Cognitive Domain.* New York: Longman.

Bourdieu, P. (1997) The Forms of Capital, in Halsey, A.H. et al. (eds.) *Education: Culture, Economy, and Society.* Oxford: Oxford University Press, pp.46-58.

Bransford, J. D. (1979) *Human Cognition: Learning, Understanding and Remembering.* Belmont, CA.: Wadsworth.

Brumfit, C. J. (1980) Seven last slogans. *Modern English Teacher*, 7(1), pp.30-1.

Bruner, J. S. and Haste, H. (eds.) (1990) *Making Sense: The Child's Construction of the World.* London: Routledge.

Buckingham, D. (2003). *Media Education: Literacy, Learning and Contemporary Culture.* Cambridge, UK: Polity.

Cameron, D. (2001). *Working with Spoken Discourse.* London: Sage.

Carter, R. & McCarthy, M. (1997) *Exploring Spoken English.* Cambridge: Cambridge University Press.

Cazden, C. B. (1988) *Classroom Discourse: the language of teaching and learning.* Portsmouth, N. H. : Heinemann.

Chalker, S. (1994) Pedagogical Grammar: Principles and Problems, in Bygate, M., Tonkyn, A. and Williams, E. (eds.) *Grammar and the Language Teacher.* Hemel Hempstead: Prentice Hall International, pp.31-44.

Cortazzi, M. and Jin, L. (1996) Cultures of Learning: Language Classrooms in China, in H. Coleman (ed.) *Society and the Language Classroom.* Cambridge: Cambridge University Press, pp.169-206.

Crystal, D. (2010) *The Cambridge encyclopedia of language.* Cambridge: Cambridge University Press.

Cunningsworth, A. (1995) *Choosing your Coursebook.* Oxford: Heinemann.

Dadds, M. (2001). Continuing professional development: nurturing the expert within, in J. Soler, A. Craft & H. Burgess (Eds.) *Teacher Development: Exploring Our Own Practice.* Milton Keynes: The Open University, pp.50-6.

Davis, P. & Rinvolucri, M. (1988) *Dictation: new methods, new possibilities.* Cambridge: Cambridge University Press.

Doff, A. (1988) *Teach English: A training course for teachers.* Cambridge: Cambridge University Press.

Dulay, H. C. and Burt, M. K. (1974) You Can't Learn without Goofing, in Richards, J. C. (ed.) *Error Analysis.* Harlow: Longman, pp.95-123.

Emmitt, M. & Pollock, J. (1997) *Language and Learning: an introduction for teaching.* (2nd edition). South Melbourne: Oxford University Press.

Evans, J. (ed.) (2004). *Literacy Moves On: Using Popular Culture, new technologies and critical literacy in the primary classroom.* London: David Fulton.

Gao, G. and Ting-Toomey, S. (1998) *Communicating effectively with the Chinese.* Thousand Oaks, CA.: Sage.

Gardner, H. (1983) *Frames of Mind: The Theory of Multiple Intelligences.* New York: Basic Books.

Gil, G. (2002) Two complementary modes of foreign language classroom interaction. *ELT Journal*, Jul 2002, 56, 3. pp.273-9.

Glenwright, P. (2002). Language Proficiency Assessment for Teachers: The Effects of Benchmarking on Writing Assessment in Hong Kong Schools. *Assessing Writing*, 33, 8, 2, pp. 84-109.

Glenwright, P. (2005). Grammar Error Strike Hard: Language Proficiency Testing of Hong Kong Teachers and The Four "Noes". *Journal of Language, Identity and Education*, 4(3), 201-226.

Graham, C. (1979) *Jazz Chants for Children*. New York: Oxford University Press.

Hall, E & Hall, C. (1988) *Human Relations in Education.* London: Routledge.

Howe, M. J. A. (1997) *IQ in Question: The Truth about Intelligence.* London: Sage Publications.

Hughes, A. (1989) *Testing for Language Teachers.* Cambridge: Cambridge University Press.

Hyland, K. (2003) *Second Language Writing.* Cambridge: Cambridge University Press.

Kenworthy, J. (1987) *Teaching English Pronunciation.* London: Longman.

Kivela, R., Glenwright, P., Snipe, P. & Alano C. (2004). *Let's Sing! A book of songs, chants and language learning activities for primary school children and their teachers.* Hong Kong: The Hong Kong Institute of Education Department of English.

Lau, S. (ed.) (1996) *Growing Up the Chinese Way: Chinese Child and Adolescent Development.* Hong Kong: Chinese University Press.

Li, J. (2003). US and Chinese Cultural Beliefs About Learning. *Journal of Educational Psychology*, 95, 2, 258-267.

Lightbown, P. M. and Spada, N. (1993) *How Languages are Learned.* Oxford: Oxford University Press.

Little, D. (1994) Words and their properties: Arguments for a lexical approach to pedagogical grammar, in Odlin, T. (ed.) *Perspectives on Pedagogical Grammar.* Cambridge: Cambridge University Press, pp.99-123

Littlewood, W. and Liu, N-f. (1996) *Hong Kong Students and Their English: LEAP.* Hong Kong: The University of Hong Kong and Macmillan.

Mahon, T. (ed.) (1999) *Using big books to teach English: units of work for the Primary Reading Project.* Hong Kong: Hong Kong Institute of Education.

Murphey, T. (1994) *Music and song.* Oxford: Oxford University Press.

Norrish, J. (1983) *Language Learners and Their Errors.* London: ELTS Macmillan.

O'Keeffe, A. McCarthy, M & Carter, R. (2007) *From Corpus to Classroom: language use and language teaching.* Cambridge: Cambridge University Press.

Paltridge, J. (2000) *Making Sense of Discourse Analysis.* Gold Coast: AEE.

Peregoy, S. E. & Boyle, O. F. (2005) *Reading, Writing and Learning in ESL: a resource book for K-12 teachers.* (4th edition). Boston, Mass.: Pearson/Allyn & Bacon.

Rowe, M. (1986) Wait time: Slowing down may be a way of speeding up. *Journal of Teacher Education*, 37: 43-50

Rutherford. W. E. (1987) *Second Language Grammar: Learning and Teaching.* London: Longman.

Sharwood Smith, M. (1988) Consciousness raising and the second language learner, in Rutherford, W and Sharwood Smith, M (eds.) *Grammar and Second Language Teaching.* Boston, MA: Heinle and Heinle, pp.51-60.

Shohamy, E. G. (2001). *The power of tests: a critical perspective on the uses of language tests.* Harlow, England: Longman.

Sinclair, J. McH. & Coulthard, R.M. (1975). *Towards an analysis of discourse: the English used by teachers and pupils.* London: Oxford University Press.

Thornbury, S. (1997) *About language: tasks for teachers of English.* New York: Cambridge University Press.

Thornbury, S. & Slade, D. (2006) *Conversation: From Description to Pedagogy.* Cambridge: Cambridge University Press.

Ting-Toomey, S, (1999) *Communicating Across Cultures.* New York: Guilford Press.

Tollefson. J. W. (ed.) (1995) *Power and Inequality in Language Education.* Cambridge: Cambridge University Press.

Tsui, A. B. M. (1993) Grammar in the Language Curriculum, in *Education Department, English Section, Advisory Inspectorate. Teaching Grammar and Spoken English: a Handbook for Hong Kong Schools.* Hong Kong: Government Printer, pp.21-30.

Tyrrell, J. (2001). *The power of fantasy in early learning.* London: Routledge/Falmer.

Van Lier, L. (1995) *Introducing Language Awareness.* Harmondsworth: Penguin.

Vygotsky, L. S. (1978) *Mind in Society. The Development of Higher Psychological Processes.* Cambridge, MA: Harvard University Press.

Walker, E. A. (1997) *Oral foreign language anxiety in Hong Kong schools: its relationship with the age-related factors, school form and self-perception.* Unpublished Ph.D. Thesis. University of Hong Kong.

Walsh, S. (2006). *Investigating Classroom Discourse.* London: Routledge.

Wang, L. & Glenwright, P. (2008). Inspiring New Perspectives: The Use of Multimedia and Other Activities in the Teaching of Linguistics. *Asian Journal of English Language Teaching*, 18, 17-40.

Watkins, D. and Biggs J. B (eds.) (1996) *The Chinese Learner: Cultural: Psychological and Contextual Influences.* Hong Kong: CERC and ACER.

Widdowson, H. G. (1978) *Teaching Language as Communication.* Oxford: Oxford University Press.

Willis, J. (1996) *A Framework for Task-Based Learning.* Harlow: Longman.

Wright, T. (1987) *Roles of Teachers and Learners.* Oxford: Oxford University Press.

In-service teachers

Petra O'Dwyer, Noeleen Haney, Edward Oosterhuizen, Bill O'Sullivan, Miranda Breding, Anne Macpherson, Samantha Reid and many others.

www.ingramcontent.com/pod-product-compliance
Lightning Source LLC
La Vergne TN
LVHW021550080426
835510LV00019B/2457